THE TABERNACLE

by

EDMONT HAINS, D.D.

Introduction by
Oswald J. Smith, LL.D., D.D., F.R.G.S.

ZONDERVAN PUBLISHING HOUSE
GRAND RAPIDS, MICHIGAN

To MARY

Introduction

The contents of this book prove the Bible to be the Word of God. This volume is indeed a mighty Christian apologetic. Edmont Hains does not offer this book as a treatise on Christian apologetics, and never employs the argumentative tone. Without even trying to do so, he simply unfolds the deep truths of the Old Testament in such a way as to prove the Bible to be God's inspired Word.

Nowhere have I encountered a study of the Tabernacle that has gripped me as this has. I was so impressed by Dr. Hains' series of messages on the Tabernacle that I had him present these studies twice in a single year at People's Church in Toronto. His ministry is unique. He is called of God to unfold the Old Testament, not only to Bible scholars and students, but to great masses of people in the largest auditoriums and tabernacles in America and Canada. He has learned the art of taking the deepest and most profound truths of the Word of God and placing these truths before his hearers in a most fascinating and enlightening manner.

May God bless this book and its author. This one volume alone is sufficient to silence forever any last moans of so-called "higher criticism" coming out of the smoldering ruins of Germany.

OSWALD SMITH, LL.D., D.D., F.R.G.S.
Pastor, People's Church, Toronto, Canada

Contents

Section I
The "Greater and More Perfect Tabernacle"

Then verily the first covenant had also ordinances of divine service, and a worldly sanctuary. For there was a tabernacle made; the first, wherein was the candlestick, and the table, and the shewbread; which is called the sanctuary. And after the second veil, the tabernacle, which is called the Holiest of all; which had the golden censer, and the ark of the covenant overlaid around about with gold, wherein was the golden pot that had manna, and Aaron's rod that budded, and the tables of the covenant; and over it the cherubims of glory shadowing the mercyseat; of which we cannot now speak particularly. Now when these things were thus ordained, the priests went always into the first tabernacle, accomplishing the service of God. But into the second went the high priest alone once every year, not without blood, which he offered for himself, and for the errors of the people: the Holy Ghost this signifying, that the way into the holiest of all was not yet made manifest, while as the first tabernacle was yet standing: which was a figure for the time then present, in which were offered both gifts and sacrifices, that could not make him that did the service perfect, as pertaining to the conscience; which stood only in meats and drinks, and divers washings, and carnal ordinances, imposed on them until the time of reformation. But Christ being come an high priest of good things to come, by a greater and more perfect tabernacle, not made with hands, that is to say, not of this building; neither by the blood of goats and calves, but by his own blood he entered in once into the holy place, having obtained eternal redemption for us. For if the blood of bulls and of goats, and the ashes of an heifer sprinkling the unclean, sanctifieth to the purifying of the flesh: how much more shall the blood of Christ, who through the eternal Spirit offered himself without spot to God, purge your conscience from dead works to serve the living God?

—HEBREWS 9:1-14

Section I: The "Greater and More Perfect Tabernacle"

"A SHADOW OF GOOD THINGS TO COME"

God called Moses and the children of Israel out of Egypt in order that He might reveal Himself to Israel and, through Israel, to the world. The world was lost in sin and darkness and ignorance; but in the quiet loneliness of the Wilderness, God showed how mankind could be saved.

Amidst the thunder and the lightning of Mt. Sinai, God gave the Ten Commandments; and on the same mountain, and in the same wilderness, and at the same time, God gave the Institution of the Wilderness Tabernacle. When God gave the Ten Commandments He showed how dreadfully lost man is because he cannot keep those holy commandments. But when God gave the Institution of the Wilderness Tabernacle and, later, His own Son of whom the Tabernacle was only a type and a shadow, He showed how wonderfully saved man could be.

God allowed Moses to look into the Heavenlies from Mt. Sinai. God "made known his ways unto Moses, his acts unto the children of Israel." From Mt. Sinai, Moses saw the entire plan of redemption and was told to put into concrete objective form the spiritual things that he saw. The Wilderness Tabernacle is the result. Moses was exhorted again and again to see that he make it according to the pattern "which was shewed thee in the mount."

In the ninth chapter of Hebrews we are told several times that the tabernacle in the Wilderness was a type and a shadow of the Lord Jesus Christ, who is called the "greater and more perfect tabernacle, not made with hands, that is

11

to say, not of this building." Moses carried out God's in-
struction so perfectly that it is easy now for us to look
at the Wilderness Tabernacle and see that in every detail
it was a type and a shadow of Jesus Christ.

THE STRUCTURE OF THE TABERNACLE

The Tabernacle was a small oblong building divided into
two parts by a veil or curtain so that the innermost part of the
Tabernacle formed a perfect cube. This innermost room
with the perfect measurements, (height, length and breadth
equal,) and made of the perfect metal, gold, was called
the Holy of Holies. It was lighted by the glory of God
and must have been a room of exquisite beauty. The outer
room of the Tabernacle was called simply, "the Holy Place."
It also had golden walls and a beautiful curtain which formed
the entrance.

In the Holy of Holies there was only one piece of furniture. This was the Golden Ark of the Covenant, an oblong
box covered with gold. The lid of the Ark was one piece of
solid gold and was called the Mercy Seat. Two golden
cheribum lay prostrate on this golden lid with their faces
toward each other. The actual presence of the Glory of
God was just over the Mercy Seat and between the faces of
the cheribum.

If we think of a huge cross lying flat on the ground, the
head of the cross would be right where the golden ark was
in the Holy of Holies. The cross beams of the cross would
be in the Holy Place and would mark the position of the
three pieces of furniture in this part of the building namely,
the Golden Candlestick on the extreme left, the Golden Altar
of Incense in the center and the Golden Table of Shewbread
at the extreme right; all three running parellel to the beautiful veil that divided the Holy Place from the Holy of Holies.

Just out in front of the Little Building was the Brazen
Laver where the priests washed themselves before going into

the Tabernacle, and on out beyond the Brazen Laver was the Brazen Altar of Sacrifice which would of course be at the foot of the cross. In other words in Exodus and Leviticus fifteen hundred years before Christ died on the cross, God almighty directed that these five pieces of furniture be placed in the form of an exact cross!

Is this a coincidence, or does the Wilderness Tabernacle actually look forward to the Lord Jesus and His cross as Hebrews IX and X declares it does?

God almighty uses less than two chapters in the Holy Bible to describe the creation of the entire universe but He uses nearly forty-five chapters in the Bible to describe the building of the Tabernacle and the services directly connected with it. Approximately thirty-five of these chapters are in Exodus and Leviticus. Starting with Exodus XXV the Tabernacle takes up nearly all the rest of the book. And beginning at Leviticus I the Tabernacle goes right on through nearly the entire book up to Chapter XXV.

The Tabernacle was very dear to the heart of God because it represented his only beloved Son and what His beloved Son would do for us. The Cross is so everlastingly important that God directed the furniture inside and outside of the Tabernacle to be placed in the form of a cross. Josephus, the first century historian, places the furniture as given here.

THE LIGHT OF THE WORLD

Let us look into the wonders of the Tabernacle and see how God could tell, in object form, about the Lord Jesus Christ long before He came to dwell in the "greater and more perfect tabernacle, not made with hands, that is to say, not of this building," in other words, long before Jesus Christ became incarnate in a body.

What does the Golden Candlestick mean? Why was it made of the perfect metal, gold?

Why did it employ the perfect number, seven? The reason is this: it was a perfect type of Jesus Christ, the Light

of the World. And why was the Table of Shewbread there?
What was the reason for having something so humble as
bread in so magnificent a building? The Table of Shewbread was a type of Jesus Christ, who said centuries later,
"I am the bread of life." Similarly, everything in the Tabernacle pointed out forward to the Lord Jesus Christ. The
Golden Altar of Incense was Jesus Christ our Intercessor,
pleading for us before the Holy of Holies of God. The
Golden Ark of the Covenant, which contained the Ten Commandments and which was in the very presence of God in
the Holy of Holies, represented Jesus Christ, who keeps the
Ten Commandments for us. The Brazen Laver, which contained the water and stood outside the little building, was
Jesus Christ, who cleanses us from sin and who is "the
water of life." And the Brazen Altar of Sacrifice was Jesus
Christ who gave Himself for us.

"HOLY, HOLY, HOLY"

No human being on earth was ever allowed to enter
through the veil into the Holy of Holies. Why? Because
God is holy and all men are sinners. There can be no possible affinity between a Holy Being and a sinful being;
hence, the veil was placed there to keep mankind from
God. By nature we are all fallen beings. Should sin
ever come into the presence of God, it would blast the universe apart. It was necessary, therefore, that this veil keep
mankind from God.

We do not realize fully the holiness of God. The light
and the presence of Jehovah are more wonderful than the
light of the sun. The sun of this solar system is ninety-three
million miles away. The light that comes to us from the sun
is so powerful that should a human being manage to come
within fifty million miles of that heavenly body, the light
of the sun (not the heat) would blow him to the four
corners of the universe.

Two sons of the high priest, Nadab and Abihu, one day

entered the Holy Place apart from God's direction and were instantly burned to cinders. It is my belief that if they had gone into the Holy of Holies the entire solar system would have blown apart with more violence than if a thousand tons of atomic energy had been released. God hates sin and anything and anybody connected with sin; and the problem which the Almighty God faced was: How can a sinner approach a holy God? To solve this problem God Almighty exhausted the resources of infinity and eventually sent the Lord Jesus Christ to die on the Cross to make it possible for sinful men to come into the presence of God.

"Not without Blood"

The great plan of atonement and redemption was foreshadowed in the services connected with the Wilderness Tabernacle. There was one exception—and only one exception— with regard to a sinner's coming into the presence of God. There was one being on the earth—and only one— who could come into the Holy of Holies, and he could come in only on one day of the year: the Day of Atonement. And he could go in under only one everlasting condition, and that condition was *blood*. Once a year, then, on the great Day of Atonement, the high priest, "not without blood, which he offered for himself, and for the [sins] of the people," entered the Holy of Holies.

What an awesome and tremendous experience that was for the high priest when he knew that he was going directly into the presence of his Creator! Do you suppose he looked at his so-called "good works"? Do you suppose he looked at the education? Do you suppose he looked at the good deeds he was going to do in the future? No, he had only one hope, he had only one virtue, and that was the blood that God had directed him to bring into the Holy of Holies and sprinkle on the Mercy Seat. Therefore, on the day that the high priest entered the Holy of Holies he had to kneel like any other miserable sinner and say:

Just as I am, without one plea,
But that Thy blood was shed for me,
And that Thou bidd'st me come to Thee,
O Lamb of God, I come! I come!

"Behold the Lamb of God"

As we continue with our study it will become increasingly clear that the Wilderness Tabernacle and everything connected with it was a type of the Lord Jesus Christ. But when one looks at the sacrificial animals themselves, and especially at the lamb, the fact becomes crystal clear. There was eleven features and specifications regarding the lamb that was offered for the sins of the people: (1) the animal had to be a lamb; (2) it had to be a male lamb; (3) it had to be the first-born of the flock; (4) it had to be without spot or blemish; (5) no bone of it could be broken; (6) it had to be tested and tempted to make sure of its perfection; (7) it had to die while young; (8) it had to die for sin vicariously; (9) its blood had to be shed to take away sin; (10) it had to be killed at "the beginning of the going down of the sun or between the evenings" (the middle of the afternoon, three o'clock, or, according to Roman time, the ninth hour); (11) the death of the lamb made it possible for a sinner to enter the presence of God.

These Tabernacle services and, later, the Temple services, continued nearly a thousand years before the Lord Jesus came to fulfill them all. When John the Baptist, who was the last and the greatest of the prophets, came, the same sacrificial services were being held in the Temple of Jerusalem, which Temple was, of course, modeled after the ancient Wilderness Tabernacle. In God's own time, in the year 30 A.D., Christ was on this earth, and when John the Baptist first saw the Lord Jesus, he cried, "Behold the Lamb of God, which taketh away the sin of the world."

Let us see how perfectly the Lord Jesus fulfilled everything foreshadowed by the sacrificial lamb, and why the book of Revelation calls Jesus Christ "the Lamb slain from the foundation of the world": (1) Jesus was a Lamb and so called by Isaiah 750 years before Christ; (2) Jesus was a male Lamb; (3) Jesus was the first-born of the flock and when Mary "brought forth her firstborn son," she "wrapped him in swaddling clothes, and laid him in a manger"; (4) Jesus was without spot and without blemish, and certainly that cannot be said of anyone else who ever lived on this earth; (5) no bone of the Lord Jesus was broken. On several occasions His enemies took up stones to stone Him, but they never actually completed the deed. The legs of the thieves, who died on either side of the Lord Jesus Christ, were broken, but the Lord Jesus was already dead when the soldiers pierced His blessed side with a spear. (6) The Lord Jesus was tested and tempted in all points like as we are, yet without sin; (7) the Lord Jesus Christ died while He was a young man; "he was cut off out of the land of the living" (Isaiah 53) when He was only thirty-three and one-half years (8) the Lord Jesus Christ died for sin in our stead; (9) the blood of Jesus Christ, God's Son, cleanses us from all sin; (10) Christ died at the ninth hour, three o'clock in the afternoon, and on the Preparation Day of the Passover; (11) the death of the Lord Jesus made atonement for us sinners, and made it possible for us to approach a holy God. Furthermore, at the very moment He died the veil before the Holy of Holies in Jerusalem was "rent in twain from the top to the bottom." (Mark 15:38)

IT IS THE BLOOD THAT MAKETH AN ATONEMENT FOR THE SOUL"

For fifteen hundred years before the Lord Jesus came there were thousands of lambs sacrificed—looking forward to the Lamb of God. The Tabernacle was taken up and taken down hundreds of times, a fact which looked forward to the "greater and more perfect tabernacle, not made with hands." The high priest entered into the presence of God hundreds of times, which foreshadowed our High Priest who

entered into "the presence of God for us." "Neither by the
blood of goats and calves, but by his own blood he entered
in once into the holy place, having obtained eternal redemption for us. For if the blood of bulls and of goats,
and the ashes of an heifer sprinkling the unclean, sanctifieth
to the purifying of the flesh: how much more shall the blood
of Christ, who through the eternal Spirit offered himself
without spot to God, purge your conscience from dead works
to serve the living God?" (Hebrews 9:12-14).

However a Modernist may dare to belittle the precious
word "blood," God Almighty has emphasized the tremendous
importance of blood, from the beginning of the Bible to the
end of the Bible, and from the beginning of time to the end
of time. No wonder a saved sinner sings, "What can wash
away my sin? Nothing but the blood of Jesus"! What other
way is there into the presence of God? "There is power
wonder-working power, in the precious blood of the Lamb."
Where else can a sinner look for power? What other power
can you contact that will make you a being fit to stand
in the presence of an Almighty God where only cherubim,
angels and arch-angels can stand? What can you do to
make yourself such a being? You could not make yourself
a being who could live even in *this* world. You had to
depend on a power outside yourself. How can you possibly
do anything to make yourself a being who can live with
God in the *eternal* world? How do you plan to get yourself
out of the coffin into which some undertaker will eventually
place you? How do you intend to get through the six feet
of earth some gravedigger is going to throw on top of you?
You have no more power to get yourself out of that casket
and live in the eternal world with God than you had to get
yourself into this world in the first place. In fact, comparatively speaking, it would be infinitely easier for you to
create yourself out of the dust of the earth and make
yourself an earthly being—it would be infinitely easier for
you to do that—than for you to re-create yourself from the

sinner that you are into a being fit to live forever with God.

It was infinitely harder even for God Almighty to make you from a sinner into a saint, than it was for Him to make you from dust into a human being. It was comparatively easy for God to create the world and to create you in the first place; it was all done by the fiat of His power. God simply said, "Let there be light," and it was so; "Let there be animals," and it was so; "Let us make man in our own image," and it was so. But God Almighty exhausted the very resources of infinity in order to save your soul, to change you from a sinner into a saint. There was no other way even for God, and you can rest assured there is no other way for you!

When the hands and the feet of the Lord Jesus Christ dropped the precious blood, the very resources of infinity were tapped. That is why the central verse of the books of Moses is Leviticus 17:11: "For the life of the flesh is in the blood: and I have given it to you upon the altar to make an atonement for your souls: for it is the blood that maketh an atonement for the soul."

In my college days, as I was preparing for the ministry, I was troubled strangely by one problem. I could not see why preachers and Sunday-school teachers were so concerned about sin. I had been reared in a sheltered environment. I knew nothing about sin; and everybody and everything seemed to be "all right." I was thinking about this one day when I was standing on Twenty-sixth Street and East River in New York City, and I heard a bell ring and a green van drove up. The back doors of the van opened, and twenty-five men who were chained to detectives got out of the van and walked down a gangplank to a little ferryboat that was to take them to Blackwell's Island for a term of imprisonment. As that procession clanked past me, I said, "Why, there it is—that's *sin!*" I had no sooner said that when another van drove up and the back doors opened. This time about twenty-five women got out. They were chained to matrons. There was one old woman in the crowd, and one young girl I will never forget as long as I live. She was a red-headed girl and her hair was disheveled. Her eyes were bleary and bloodshot. She had a cut on her left cheek and she was smoking a cigarette butt. As that procession filed past me, I said again, "Why there it is—*sin!*"

On that very corner stands Bellevue Hospital, that great monument to sin and misery and agony where literally thousands of people suffer on beds of pain. Much of the sickness and the suffering in that particular hospital is the result directly or indirectly, of sin. Let us look at one ward. It is about a hundred feet long and fifty feet wide. There are scores of little white beds on rubber wheels, and lying on these beds are tiny babies who will be blind because of the sins of their parents. Stand in that ward with me and say as I said, "There it is again—*sin!*"

Directly across from Bellevue Hospital the old morgue of New York City once stood. A large square yellow building, almost a perfect cube, it is no longer there. That day I had to go into the morgue to identify a body. From Manhattan, Brooklyn and the Bronx the unidentified bodies were brought nightly to that morgue. I did not want to go into such a building, but I could not escape the experience. I described the man for whom I was looking. The keeper of the morgue began to pull out the crypts, or drawers, where the bodies were kept, and as he pulled each out he would ask, "Is this him? . . . Is this him? . . . Is this him?"

He had shown me eight bodies. I did not find the body I sought but I learned a powerful lesson. One of the boys still had the marks of the ropes around his neck. An old man had a purple hole in his right temple where a bullet had pierced. Another victim had his throat slashed from ear to ear. I said almost aloud, "There it is, God. There is *sin.*"

How does sin look to the God who made the lily of the valley, and the rainbow, and the rosebush; who sits upon the Great White Throne; before whose face the earth and the heavens flee away; before whom is the glassy sea, and the four and twenty elders, and the four living creatures, who cease not day and night to cry, "Holy, holy, holy, Lord God Almighty"? How does sin look to God? The question is not how sin looks to you, or to a magazine editor, or to a Modernist preacher, but how sin looks to the God who dwells in the Holy of Holies.

ALL UNRIGHTEOUSNESS IS SIN

You may say to me, "You've seen some awful demonstrations of sin, but in our circles we don't have sin such as you've seen." Remember—*all sin is sin.* All unrighteousness is sin. Sin is usually pictured dramatically, and the moment the word "sin" is used, most people picture some fellow in a saloon singing "Sweet Adeline." But Judas Iscariot was never in a saloon, and the scribes and the Pharisees never sang "Sweet Adeline," and some Modernist preachers who are damning America never drank whiskey. Sin may take the form of drinking. But that is only one form. There are thousands of forms that sin assumes. When it takes the form of murder, it is a horrible thing. But when it takes the form of adultery, it is just as horrible. And when it takes the form of pride, or ambition, or any form of selfishness, it is just as horrible. If a thing is not right, it is wrong. If a thing is not good, it is bad. If a thing is not straight, it is crooked. "Whatsoever is not of [God] is *sin.*"

If I hold up a jar of water, the chemist will tell me that it is H_2O in liquid form. Suppose that I take that jar of water outside and let is freeze, and say, "Now, Professor, that H_2O is something different. See how hard it is." "Yes," the professor replies, "you have changed its form, haven't you?" Then I ask, "But now, sir, isn't it ice?" And the professor answers, "You have given it another name, haven't you?" Then I put the ice in a kettle on the stove and let it boil, and I say to the professor, "Now it certainly is something else. Look at the fleecy clouds going up to the ceiling, Professor!" He nods. "I see you have changed its form again." I insist, "But, sir is it not steam now?" He replies, "I see you have changed its name again, but it is still H_2O, in another form."

Whether H_2O takes the form of a liquid, or a solid, or a gas, it is still H_2O, regardless of the form it takes or the name you give it. Whether sin takes the form of adultery, murder, hate, pride, lying, stealing, ambition, or covetousness, it is still *sin*.

"They Shall Be As White As Snow"

John D. Rockefeller came to the time in his life when an unsolved problem threatened to curtail the development of the Standard Oil Company. A filthy black soot was produced in the refining of gasoline, and this soot had become a problem to the Standard Oil Company because they did not know what to do with it and they had no place to put it. The company had already bought acres of ground and tried to pile this soot in great black mountains on the ground, but this solution to the problem proved impractical. They tried pouring it into the rivers, but it floated on the surface, and at low tide for hundreds of miles the banks were made black and slimy. They even tried to burn it with superheated furnaces, but the soot went up in black clouds and under certain atmospheric conditions came down as black rain. As a last resort the research department was directed to spend six weeks seeking a solution for the black-soot problem. Before four weeks had passed the old chemist of the Standard Oil Company came into the office of John D. Rockefeller to report success. He laid an oblong block of something wrapped in white tissue paper on John D. Rockefeller's desk, and he told the great industrialist to unwrap the package. When Rockefeller did so, there lay on his desk the first cake of snow-white paraffin, or parawax, made, by the chemist's own original formula, from the despised soot.

Though your sins be as scarlet,
They shall be as white as snow;
Though they be red like crimson,
They shall be as wool.

"Darkness over All the Land unto the Ninth Hour"

Here is one of the most wonderful truths of our study. God ordained that the Passover Lamb be slain on the fourteenth day of the first month (Nisan,—March-April). The Lamb was slain and *prepared* on that day; therefore the day was called "The Preparation Day." Not only was the day of the month ordained, but the time of the day "Ye shall kill it in the evening" (Exodus 12:6) so the lamb could be roasted and eaten that *night* (Exodus 12:8). The *night* was of course the Passover *Day* because the Hebrew day began at sunset.

The exact day of the month, the exact month, and the exact time of the day of the month for the slaying of the Lamb was therefore ordained fifteen hundred years before "Christ our *Passover* is sacrificed for us" (I Cor. 5:7)! The day, month, time of day were as follows: (1) fourteenth day of the month; (2) the first month, namely March April; (3) killed "in the evening." The Hebrew here as elsewhere reads "between the evenings." It was mid-afternoon, or three o'clock. Sometimes the time is set for "the going down of the sun." That does not mean the setting of the sun. It means the time when the sun starts to go down on its way to the horizon.

Our blessed Lord Jesus died on (1) the fourteenth day; (2) of the first month March April; (3) at three o'clock which according to Roman time was "the ninth hour" on "the preparation day" (Matt. 27:46; John 19:42). No wonder the Holy Spirit in I Corinthians 5:7 says "Christ our *Passover* is sacrificed for us" and in I Peter 1:18 we are told that we are "Redeemed by the precious blood of Christ as of a Lamb without blemish and without spot *which was verily ordained before the foundation of the world.*"

The moment our Lord died on the cross "the veil of the Temple was rent in twain from top to bottom" (Mark 15:28). When this veil was rent the glorious Holy of Holies was completely opened and a way was made for sinful men to come into the presence of a Holy God! Also at the moment of our Lord's death the terrible darkness which was over the face of the whole earth "from the sixth hour to the ninth hour" lifted and *light* came to the world (Matt. 27:45).

On the preparation Day of the Passover every Jewish father killed and prepared a Passover lamb, and he did this at the proper time, "between the evenings." The high priest, standing by the Brazen Altar of sacrifice in front of the Temple, gave the signal for all Israel to kill their lambs. Therefore, even though the miserable Caiaphas (High Priest A.D. 33) would have given his very soul to stand near the dying Jesus until Christ had breathed the last painful breath, he could not have been there at that wonderful moment because he was the high priest that year, and he would have to be at the Brazen Altar of Sacrifice in front of the Temple in order to give the signal for the killing of the Passover lamb.

What a day that was for Caiaphas and for all the devils in hell and on earth! Before Pilate had awakened from his swinish slumber, Caiaphas had led the mob to the palace of Pilate to demand the death sentence. Pilate was afraid to try the case, and sent them to Herod. Herod dared not try the case, and sent them back to Pilate. By this time the crowd had been increasing to tens of thousands and all along the line of march the miserable Caiaphas was vindicating himself and hurling accusations at the precious Lord Jesus. But the supreme hour for the vindication of all hell came when the weak Pilate at last gave in and signed the death warrant of Christ.

Waving this Roman order high above his wicked head, Caiaphas led the way throughout the Via Dolorosa and on out to Golgotha, screaming, blaspheming, shouting accusations against Jesus, "Here He comes, the King of the Jews! Here He comes! Not that first—he is just a common thief. Not the last one—he is another thief. But the one between. There He is, the One who is greater than our father Abraham —the One who would destroy the Temple and build it again in three days—the One before whom you threw the palm branches on Sunday last—the One to whom you listened instead of your holy priest. Come all to Calvary! We shall see! We shall see!"

At long last they reach Golgotha. It is nine A.M. It takes but a few terrible minutes to nail the Lord Jesus to the Cross, a few more terrible minutes to sink the Cross with a sickening thud into the ground, and then that evil Caiaphas resumes his fiendish onslaughts. "Hail, King of the Jews! . . . Thou that destroyest the temple, and buildest it in three days . . . come down from the cross."

Has this beast Caiaphas no feeling? Can he not let the dying Christ alone now? Caiaphas has been screaming and blaspheming since dawn, but he is far from weary. But at twelve o'clock he begins at last to lose his crowd.

Why does the crowd start to leave at twelve o'clock? Is it because of the black darkness that settled upon the earth from the sixth to the ninth hour? That is one reason, but there is another. Remember that it is the Preparation Day for the killing of the Passover lamb, and every Jewish father must be in front of his house by the ninth hour. Therefore, many of the men started to leave, and by one o'clock most of them have gone. By two o'clock nearly all have left, and only the soldiers and the women remain near the Cross. It is very quiet there now. Caiaphas is silent at last. The bodies on the crosses have been exhausted into silence. One can hear the *drop, drop, drop* of the blood.

But now Caiaphas himself must go. Is this not the Day of the Preparation of the Passover? Is he not the high priest? Is he not the one of all Israel to give this signal for the killing of the Passover lamb? Yet, he must go. He has a job to do. He has a great honor. He must go. So Caiaphas lifts his bloody, wicked skirts and hobbles over the rough ground of Golgotha, down the hill through the darkness across the dark valley; up the hill, into the Holy City, through the Temple gate to the Brazen Altar of Sacrifice. The fire is burning at the Altar. The Levite is there with the Passover lamb. The usual questions are asked by the priest: "Is it a lamb?" "Is it the first-born of the flock?" "Is it without blemish?" "Has a bone ever been broken?" "Is it a young lamb?"

"AND THE VEIL OF THE TEMPLE WAS RENT"

It is nearing the hour of three o'clock, so the Levite answers the questions impatiently and quickly and then hands the high priest the gleaming knife. It is five minutes before three and the high priest holds the knife over the throat of the spotless lamb, while out there on the Cross the Lamb of God has already cried, "I thirst," and "My God, my God, why hast thou forsaken me?" But there is one more cry to come from that Cross; and just as the high priest draws the knife across the throat of the little lamb, that cry comes. The thunder rolls, the earth quakes, the rocks are rent, the lightning flashes, and Jesus cries with a loud voice, "It is finished." The veil of the Temple is rent "from the top to the bottom," and light comes back to the world.

Do you understand that? Do you understand that a way was made for you to come back to God? Something was done, something that happened at the heart of the universe and made it possible for God to transform a sinner into a saint. Something has been done for you. Christianity is not a religion of words. Christianity is the religion of a deed! Something happened which affected the heart of the universe from its center to its circumference, and it was done for *you*.

When the time comes for you—and it will come, should the Lord tarry—and you are lying on your bed from which you will never rise, and the doctor or the nurse whispers as kindly as possible that you will not see the morning, if you are a Christian, you can smile and say, "It is all right. Something has been done for me." If someday you are rolled into an operating room in a hospital, and the nurse explains why you and your wife or husband sign certain papers relieving the hospital of any responsibility in your case, you can smile and say, "It is all right. Something has been done for me." But only if you are a Christian can you have this assurance.

SECTION II

"The Word Became Flesh"

Whereupon neither the first testament was dedicated without blood. For when Moses had spoken every precept to all the people according to the law, he took the blood of calves and of goats, with water, and scarlet wool, and hyssop, and sprinkled both the book, and all the people, saying, This is the blood of the testament which God hath enjoined unto you. Moreover he sprinkled with blood both the Tabernacle, and all the vessels of the ministry. And almost all things are by the law purged with blood; and without shedding of blood is no remission. It was therefore necessary that the pattern of things in the heavens should be purified with these; but the heavenly things themselves with better sacrifices than these. For Christ is not entered into the holy places made with hands, which are the figures of the true; but into heaven itself, now to appear in the presence of God for us: nor yet that he should offer himself often, as the high priest entereth into the holy place every year with blood of others; for then must he often have suffered since the foundation of the world: but now once in the end of the world hath he appeared to put away sin by the sacrifice of himself. And as it is appointed unto men once to die, but after this the judgment: so Christ was once offered to bear the sins of many; and unto them that look for him shall he appear the second time without sin unto salvation.

—HEBREWS 9:18-28

Section II: "The Word Became Flesh"

THE SHADOW OF THE CROSS

As we have indicated, you will find it easy to remember the position of the furniture inside and outside the Wilderness Tabernacle if you will picture a cross lying flat on the ground. At the head of the cross in the Holy of Holies is the Golden Ark of the Covenant. On the right hand of the cross, in the Holy Place, is the Golden Candlestick. At the intersection of the crossbeams, still in the Holy Place, is the Golden Altar of incense, and on the left hand of the cross is the Golden Table of Shewbread. Just outside the little building, and toward the foot of the cross, is the Brazen Laver, and farther beyond at the foot of the cross, is the Brazen Altar of Sacrifice.

In the thirty-nine books of the Old Testament we see the shadow of the Cross, but in the Gospels the Cross is no longer a shadow, and is not horizontal, but vertical! "I, if I be lifted up . . . will draw all men unto me."

I once attended a lecture on the cosmic ray, and the professor told a little girl to go to the platform and stand sideways with her head toward the moving-picture screen. Then the lecturer directed the cosmic ray toward the little girl's head so that her profile was silhouetted on the screen. He then told the child to step aside and instructed us to to see how long the shadow of the little girl's face remained on the screen after she had gone. We were amazed to find that the shadow stayed there for five seconds after the object had left. This reveals the power of the cosmic ray.

But the light that comes from heaven and shines upon

the Cross of Jesus Christ is so powerful that it cannot only hold the shadow of the Cross two thousands years after the Cross has been taken down: it can throw the shadow of the Cross four thousand years before the Cross was erected on the hill of Calvary!

"THE WORD WAS MADE FLESH, AND DWELT AMONG US"

In Exodus 25:8 God states the primary purpose for the building of the Tabernacle. It was to be put up in the center of the camp so that the people could know that God could dwell among them. In other words, it was to prepare the human mind for the stupendous truth of the incarnation of God. God dwelt in ancient days in this Tabernacle made with hands, but when God came into the body of the Lord Jesus, He dwelt in the "greater and more perfect tabernacle, not made with hands, that is to say, not of this building" (Hebrews 9:11).

You will see how the Tabernacle was a perfect type and symbol of the Incarnation. The Tabernacle was portable; it was taken from place to place throughout the Wilderness.

When God came to dwell in the "greater and more perfect tabernacle, not made with hands," He dwelt in the portable tabernacle of the body of the Lord Jesus, who went from place to place only according to God's direction.

The Wilderness Tabernacle moved at the order of God, who directed its moving from place to place by means of a pillar of cloud by day and a pillar of fire by night. The "greater and more perfect tabernacle, not made with hands," moved only at the direction of God, and finally God directed Him to go to the Cross for us.

Although the Wilderness Tabernacle was exquisitely beautiful on the inside, it had an extremely plain exterior. It was covered with brown badger skins and from the outside it looked like any of the other buildings or tents of the Israelites because it was constructed of earthly material. Christ looked like other men from the *outside* because He was bone of our bone and flesh of our flesh, but He was entirely different from other men on the *inside* because in Him dwelt "all the fulness of the Godhead bodily."

With the possible exception of the Temple at Jerusalem, the interior of the Wilderness Tabernacle was the most exquisitely and extravagantly beautiful building that has existed in this world. The walls of both the Holy place and the Holy of Holies were of gold. The ceilings and the curtains were of the most beautiful colors and fabrics—blue, purple, scarlet, white fine-twined linen—and all of it embroidered with actual gold embroidery in the design of the heavenly cherubim.

No light from the outside world could enter the Tabernacle, and the light from the Shekinah glory on the Golden Ark of the Covenant in the Holy of Holies reflected on the golden walls and on the lovely ceiling and veil: In the Holy Place the light came from the seven Golden Candlesticks and lit the Golden Table of Shewbread and the Golden Altar of Incense, and it shed its soft light on the magnificently blended colors of blue, purple, scarlet and white fine-twined linen. It must have been unspeakably beautiful.

But have you noticed something strange? Did God make a mistake? Was the Divine Architect of the Universe so careless as to forget to put a floor in the Tabernacle? Or did He omit it purposely? Any woman knows that a rug can transform any room in an instant. Why was there no floor, or even a rug, in the Wilderness Tabernacle? The Egyptians and the Orientals made the most beautiful rugs in all the world. All the ranking officers in the Oriental armies had beautiful rugs in their tents, not only for beauty but for utility.

Have you discovered why there was no floor in the Tabernacle? God certainly did not overlook this point, but He wanted something more than beauty in the Tabernacle, and He was teaching a truth. God knew that the only floor in that beautiful Tabernacle was dirt: the sands of the Wilderness; the dirt that brings forth thorns and thistles; the dirt that has received the blood of righteous Abel and the blood of millions of men and women murdered on and off the battlefields. That was the only floor in this magnificent Tabernacle. God knew that very well, because in Numbers 5 He gave instructions as to what a priest should do when an Israelite wife proved unfaithful. The priest was to go into the Tabernacle, and pick up some of the floor of the Tabernacle, mix it with water at the Brazen Laver, and then throw it at the adulterous wife and curse her seven times.

Why was there no floor in the Tabernacle? There is a beautiful and subtle reason. The Tabernacle, among other things, is a type of the incarnation of God; and in the incarnation that God demonstrated for this world, God came *all the way down* to the earth where we live. He did not come part of the way to the stratosphere, like an angel, or a seraphim. He came *all the way down* to this old earth where you and I dwell. In other words, the Tabernacle without a floor was a perfect type of the perfect incarnation of God, who actually became man and dwelt on this sin-cursed earth.

The first temptation which the devil hurled at Christ after forty days of hunger in the Wilderness was simply this: "Do not make this a real incarnation. It is all right for You to become partially human, but You must not go all the way. You do not have to feel hunger as human beings do; You can make bread out of stones right now and satisfy Your hunger."

But the Lord Jesus knew that He came to this earth to save us from real sin and real hell, and therefore a real incarnation and a real atonement were absolutely necessary. Christ "being in the form of God, thought it not robbery to be equal with God: but made himself of no reputation . . . and was made in the likeness of men: and being found in fashion as a man, he humbled himself, and became obedient unto death, even the death of the cross" (Philippians 2:6-8).

Let us see how complete and absolute the Incarnation was. The winds of the desert and the Wilderness blew around the ancient Tabernacle, just as they blew around all the other tents and buildings of the Israelites. But everything was calm and beautiful inside the Holy Tabernacle. So also did the winds of temptation blow around the Lord Jesus Christ, but everything within was serene and beautiful. He was "in all points tempted like as we are, yet without sin."

When the Bible says He was tempted in all points like as we are, the word means exactly what it says. Does it mean He was tempted physically? Certainly it does. "Make bread out of these stones"—what is that but physical temptation and an appeal to physical passions? Was He tempted mentally? Certainly He was. "Fall down off the pinnacle of the Temple and the people will applaud you"—this must have been a severe temptation to the Lord Jesus. It was aimed at His pride—if there were one drop of pride in Him. The devil meant that He was to come floating down from the Temple and gain immediate acceptance and applause from the people. But the Lord Jesus resisted this appeal and took the lowly, humble way of a Galilean peasant. The third temptation in the Wilderness was aimed at the spiritual nature of Christ: "Fall down and worship me," said the devil, "and I will give you the kingdoms of the world." "All points . . . like as we are"—body, mind, spirit. The Lord Jesus Christ came all the way down to this earth, just as the old Wilderness Tabernacle rested upon this cursed earth. and dwelt among us."

There was no beautiful floor; there was no beautiful carpet. Christ came *all the way down*—"the Word was made *flesh,*

But perhaps you are still wondering whether or not Christ became absolutely human, and you ask, "Did He ever get tired? Did He ever get hungry and thirsty as we do?" He was very tired, according to the fourth chapter of John: "Jesus therefore, being wearied with his journey, sat thus by the well" while his disciples went into the city to buy food. On another occasion he was so tired that he fell asleep on a fishing trip in the middle of the afternoon. A young man in his early thirties must be very tired to do that. Mark tells us that the Lord was so tired that "he was in the hinder part of the ship, asleep on a pillow." He fell so sound asleep that when a sudden thunderstorm arose it did not awaken Him. The lightning flashed, the thunder rolled, the little fishing boat heaved to and fro upon the bosom of the tempestuous sea, but the tired Man slept on. The rest of the disciples were excitedly working with the sails and the rudder; but this did not awaken the tired Man. Finally they had to shake Him and say,

> Carest Thou not that we perish?
> How canst Thou lie asleep;
> When each moment so madly is threat'ning
> A grave in the angry deep?

I can picture our blessed Lord coming out of a deep sleep in the midst of the thundering storm, and smiling. Perhaps He smiled then and said, "Well, you certainly are terribly frightened," and then added, with words that we poor humans can understand now, "But am I not in the same boat with you? Your garments are wet, but Mine are not dry, either."

Yes, our Lord Jesus knew what it was to be tired. He knew what it was to be hungry, and He knew what it was to be thirsty. One of the last seven words spoken in the darkness from the Cross of Golgotha was "I thirst"; and be it said to the everlasting condemnation of sinful man that in that terrible moment there was not even a cup of cold water for Him who had created all the streams and the brooks and the rivers in the world.

Consider further the Incarnation. It was a complete incarnation. Christ became absolutely human. Our Lord knew moments and hours of sorrow, but during most of His life He was a radiantly happy young man. No matter how medieval art has emphasized the sorrow of Christ (and He knew sorrow as no man has ever known it), we still have an entirely different picture of the Lord Jesus Christ presented in the Gospels. He loved little children. He loved the birds and the sunsets. He was invited to weddings and parties and dinners. In fact, most of His addresses in the Gospel of Luke are really after-dinner speeches. He attended suppers frequently. Simon made Him a feast. Zacchaeus made Him a feast. Martha and Mary made Him a feast.

He began His public ministry at a wedding at Cana of Galilee, and people in the Orient exercise care in issuing invitations to wedding feasts because it is not easy to get rid of an undesirable guest. Such feasts lasted five or six days, and even longer. But Jesus and His disciples and His mother were *invited* to the feast, and after a day or two of feasting, their supply of refreshments was exhausted. Did the Lord Jesus stand and declare in a gloomy voice, "Let us all go home now. We have had enough of this feasting"? He most certainly did not. He created more refreshments then and there when He turned twelve water pots of water into twelve great water pots of wine.

Of course, the scribes and the Pharisees noticed all this, and they became angry and jealous—perhaps because they never were invited to these suppers and dinners. So the scribes and the Pharisees started a scandal about the jubilant Lord Jesus and circulated the story that He was "a gluttonous man, and a winebibber, a friend of publicans and sinners." Of course, that was a gross slander and lie. The scribes and the Pharisees asked another scheming question: "John the Baptist told you fellows to fast, but this Jesus whom you are now following—does He teach you to fast? Go ask Him about that."

I can prove that our Saviour smiled. For example, when the disciples came to Him with the question asked by the Pharisee. Very likely the disciples had a worried look that amused the Lord Jesus, so He went directly to the scribes and the Pharisees, and on this one occasion, at least, He employed wit and satire. In substance, this is what Christ said to His critics: "Now, you fellows are worrying too much. You are constantly engaged in the business of picking little splinters out of other people's eyes. Now, if you intend to keep on in this business, I am going to show you a new technique, and here it is: take first the beam out of your own eye, and then you can see more clearly to take the splinter out of your brother's eye." Imagine the amusement that rippled across the crowd when the Lord Jesus made this declaration to the long-robed, long-bearded, long-faced scribes and Pharisees. The Lord Jesus went even further when He said, "John the Baptist came neither eating nor drinking, and you did not want him. I come eating and drinking, and you do not want Me. What do you want? You are like children sitting in the market place, saying, 'We have piped unto you, and ye have not danced' " (Luke 7:31-35).

Do you know that the Lord Jesus sang on at least one occasion? That occasion was at the Table of the Last Supper. Scripture tells us that "when they had sung an hymn, they went out into the mount of Olives." And we know that on this occasion they sang one of the two regular Passover songs.

But I can eclipse everything I have said about the humanity of our Lord by quoting just one verse, the verse which is alleged to be the shortest in the Bible, John 11:35: "Jesus wept." Now I know He was really human; and when I look into the reason for His weeping as it is recorded in the story of the raising of Lazarus, I am more convinced than ever that He was human.

Why did He weep on the way to the grave of Lazarus? He knew very well that the people who were following Him were going to be very happy before the day was over, and that Lazarus was going to be alive again. But the point is, Martha and Mary and the rest of the people were not happy *then*. They were weeping *then*, and because they were weeping *then*, and for no other reason than that they were weeping *then,* "Jesus wept."

We have not a high priest who is not touched with the feelings of our infirmities, but one who "was in all points tempted like as we are, yet without sin." Do you ever question whether Christ understands you now? Do you ever question whether the great God knows about your broken heart and whether He cares? "Jesus wept."

> Somebody knows when your heart aches,
>   And ev'rything seems to go wrong;
> Somebody knows when the shadows
>   Need chasing away with a song;
> Somebody knows when you're lonely,
>   Tired, discouraged and blue;
> Somebody wants you to know Him,
>   And know that He dearly loves you.

Wood and Gold

If I were to stop here, I would have no message for you or for myself or for anybody. I would be absolutely "messageless," and, furthermore, I would have a Wilderness Tabernacle made only and entirely of wood, because the wood in the Wilderness Tabernacle represents the humanity of our Lord. Incidentally, it was acacia wood, the wood that grows in the desert like "a root out of dry ground." "He hath no form nor comeliness, and when we shall see him, there in no beauty that we should desire him."

But the wooden boards of the Tabernacle walls were covered with magnificent gold, and the gold represents the deity of our Lord. This is seen very plainly when one considers the Golden Ark inside the Holy of Holies. The sides and the bottom of the Ark were made of wood covered with gold, and the lid of the Ark was of solid gold and was called the Mercy Seat. That the Ark in the Holy of Holies was intended by God to foreshadow Christ is clear from the fact that it kept something for us that no one else could keep; and that something was the Law. The Ten Commandments were inside the Ark. Also inside that Ark was a pot of manna which represented the Lord Jesus as the Bread of Life. And Aaron's rod that budded. How does one get a rod? It must be cut from a tree, and this fact was a type of the death of Christ. But did you notice that this rod budded and blossomed? This was a type of the resurrection of the Lord Jesus.

The Wilderness Tabernacle was not made only of wood. The wood was covered with *gold*. The wood is a type of our *Lord's* humanity. The gold typifies *His Diety*. Jesus Christ was more than human. A merely human Christ would be of absolutely no avail for me. Christ was beautifully human—we grant this; Socrates and Abraham Lincoln were also beautifully human. But after life's fitful fever they sleep well. When it is time for me to be put in my coffin and placed in my grave, and when I am six feet under the sod, what good will a human Christ be to me? I need someone—and I *have* someone—who can reach down through that dirt, take my hand with the grip of the Lion of the Tribe of Judah, and say, "Come forth."

Christ was weeping at the grave of Lazarus. He commanded the stone to be rolled away, but even Mary and Martha interfered and said, "By this time he stinketh; for he hath been dead four days." The Lord Jesus rebuked them sweetly by declaring, "I am the resurrection, and the life: he that believeth in me, though he were dead, yet shall he live: and whosoever liveth and believeth in me shall never die." Then they rolled away the stone and the Son of God cried, "Lazarus, come forth." And "he that was dead came forth, bound hand and foot with graveclothes."

Jesus wept. What was He as He stood there weeping by the tomb? He was very man of very man. But what was Christ when He cried, "Lazarus, come forth?" Then Christ was very God of very God. What was Christ when He was asleep with His head on a pillow during the storm on Galilee? He was very man of very man. But what was Christ when He stood on the deck on the ship and cried to the wind and the waves, "Peace, be still"? Then He was very God of very God. That is why the Wilderness Tabernacle was made of wood, symbolizing the humanity of Jesus, and gold, representing His deity.

It is true that Jesus Christ was very God of very God, but in order to save us from real sin, and from a real Satan, and from a real hell, He had to become completely incarnate and make a complete atonement. When it came time for Him to thirst, He thirsted. When it came time for Him to hunger, He hungered. When it came time for Him to suffer, He suffered. To do less must have been a keen temptation to Him. But, thank God, He went all the way. He came all the way down. The Tabernacle had no floor.

The last keen temptation that the devil hurled at Christ was through a group of kindhearted women who offered Him a cup of wine mixed with myrrh, just as He was marching up to Golgotha to be crucified. Wine and myrrh in combination form an anesthetic, or an opiate. Even Roman severity allowed this merciful portion to be given to condemned criminals, but when our Lord "tasted thereof, he would not drink." Why? Because He was going to pay the full price for our salvation. There was something about the Atonement that made it necessary for our Lord to "go the limit" in order to save us from real sin, and a real Satan, and a real hell. Our Lord had to feel real nails and real wounds in real hands and feet. The agony of the Crucifixion could not be dulled. He came all the way down to this old earth. There was no floor in the Wilderness Tabernacle.

Beside a lake in New Jersey the Y.M.C.A. has a boy's camp. One day a contest was held to see which boy could touch the bottom of the lake, which was nearly twenty feet deep. One little fellow dived in and stayed down nearly a minute. When he came up he said rather doubtfully to the judges, "I think I've touched it, sir, but I'm not sure." A second little fellow dived in, stayed down a minute and said, "I'm pretty sure I touched it." And a third little fellow dived in and stayed down ninety seconds. The lifeguard feared for the little fellow and was about to dive in for him when the lad's head bobbed above the surface. He could hardly gasp, but in his uplifted hand he held a handful of mud from the floor of the lake, and the judges had no doubt that he had touched the bottom.

When the Lord Jesus Christ came from heaven He came all the way down. He touched this dirty old earth, and when He went back through the clouds into heaven carrying a poor lost thief in His bosom nobody in heaven or hell had any doubt but what the Incarnation had been complete.

"JESUS PAID IT ALL"

However, the Incarnation was only part of the price that the Lord Jesus paid to redeem us. The full price was so terrible that it had to be paid in at least five installments, mentioned in Philippians: (1) Christ thought that being on an equality with God was not a thing to be grasped after; (2) in order to save us from sin, He made Himself of no reputation; (3) He was made in the likeness of sinful man; (4) "Being found in fashion as a man, he became obedient unto death."

But do not think the price of the Atonement has by any means been paid in those four terrible and wonderful installments. There is another installment, the fifth: "even the death of the cross."

Our Lord Jesus paid the first four installments without the slightest hesitation. But when He was to pay the fifth installment, "even the death of the cross," Christ hesitated and wavered. This fifth installment was foreshadowed in two of the most poignant services connected with the Wilderness Tabernacle.

I say our Lord Jesus Christ hesitated and wavered before paying this fifth and last installment because a study of the last twenty-four hours of His life reveals this to be a fact. During this period of His life our Lord uses the first personal pronoun, gives expression to His own feelings, pleads for pity and companionship, and asks the Father, "If it be possible, let this cup pass from me."

We are going to tread on holy ground now as we listen to our Lord and watch Him during those last twenty-four hours of His life. He uses the first personal pronoun differently, and gives expression to His own feelings in a manner He never employed prior to that last terrible day.

Listen to Him: "With desire I have desired to eat this passover with you before I suffer." "My soul is exceeding sorrowful unto death." "Tarry ye here, and watch with me." "What, could ye not watch with me one hour?" The agony our Lord faces is so terrible that we see Him asking help and begging aid from poor fishermen like Peter, James and John!

A short time ago we heard the Son of God cry, "Come unto me . . . and I will give you rest," and "Look unto me, and be ye saved, all the ends of the earth." Now He is asking man for help.

He goes deeper into the Garden now, and Mark is the only Gospel writer who uses the term regarding Jesus which makes his statement one of the most poignant in the Bible. The most awesome sentence in Scripture is, of course, "My God, my God, why hast thou forsaken me?" but a soul-shaking sentence is used by Mark to describe the agony of Jesus as our Lord approached the crucial hour: "He . . . began to be sore *amazed*."

> Into the woods my Master went,
> Clean forspent, forspent.
> Into the woods my Master came,
> Forspent with grief and shame.
> But the olives they were not blind to Him,
> The little gray leaves were kind to Him:
> The thorn-tree had a mind to Him
> As into the woods He came.

Then followed the bloody sweat and agony as He cried to His Father, "O my Father, if it be possible, let this cup pass from me." Over and over again our Lord made this moving request: "Let this cup pass from me!"

What cup? Of what was He thinking? Was it death? No. He would have died more quickly and easily than any soldier in the Roman army. Was it the agony and the torture of crucifixion? No. He could have endured that with more fortitude than any soldier in Caesar's Tenth Legion. What was it then?

You can understand the answer only when you read II Corinthians 5:21: "For he hath made him to be sin for us, who knew no sin; that we might be made the righteousness of God in him." He who knew no sin *became* sin for us. And then read I Peter—He "his own self bare our sins in his own body on the tree," and, again, Isaiah 53:6: "The Lord hath *laid on him* the iniquity of us all."

Do you see the wonderful truth? Our Lord Jesus not only bore the penalty for our sins: He *bore our sins!* He not only took the punishment for our sin: He *took our sin!* He "his own self bare our sins in his own body on the tree."

> Up that Calvary road, 'neath a terrible load,
> Walked a man with a cross and a crown;
> And the cross that He bore, and the crown that He wore,
> With deep agony weighted Him down.
> For the cross was an emblem of sin and of blame,
> And the crown made of thorns was a circlet of shame,
> For the sins of the world on His shoulders were hurled
> On that blood-sprinkled Calvary road.
>
> Up the Calvary road, through the mob's cruel goad,
> To the brow of the hill He was led;
> And the sun hid its face, and the earth reeled a-pace,
> While His friends in dread terror had fled.
> But the pains that were His when the nails pierced Him through
> Were as nothing compared with the anguish He knew
> When the sins of the world on His shoulders were hurled
> On that blood-sprinkled Calvary road.

The Lord knew this to be the deeper truth of the Atonement, and in the wonderful Wilderness Tabernacle and the services connected therewith He foreshadowed it plainly and wonderfully. The priests went down to the Brazen Altar of Sacrifice to receive the spotless little lamb, and there shed its atoning blood. But first the priest raised his hands over the people and over himself and then rested his hands upon the head of the innocent lamb.

What was the priest doing? He was setting aside the lamb for the sacrifice, but when he puts his hands on the head of the little lamb, he was doing something more. He was symbolically transferring the sins of the people and of himself to that innocent lamb. He "his own self bare our sins in his own body on the tree."

To make this tremendous truth still plainer our God directed in the Wilderness Tabernacle services the following ritual, which foreshadows the two great aspects of the atoning work of Christ. The first aspect of the Atonement is that our Lord took the penalty *for* our sins; and the second aspect is that He actually *took our sins* into and upon His own body. That explains why He cried in the Garden, "O my Father, if it be possible, let this cup pass from me." It also explains that expression "sore amazed" which Mark uses to describe the soul-agony of Jesus on His way into Gethsemane, and it also suggests an additional explanation of that terrible cry which came through the darkness from the Cross: "My God, my God, why hast thou forsaken me?"

Here is the ritual which forshadows the second aspect of the Atonement. Two he-goats, without spot or blemish and with no bone broken, and all the other numerous features necessary to foreshadow the perfect sacrifice of the Lord Jesus, were brought to the high priest before the Altar of Sacrifice. The high priest laid his hands again upon one of the goats as he had on the little lamb, and then the goat was sacrificed. But the second goat, which was called the "scapegoat," required a different service. The hands of the priest were raised above the congregation and above himself and then laid on the head of the scapegoat, but in order to foreshadow the second aspect of the atonement of Christ, the scapegoat, with the sins *on* its innocent head, was led by a Levite out of the court into the Wilderness and into the Land of Nod, never to come back! Thus the second aspect of the Atonement was clearly foreshadowed, and it is that taking of our sins into His own body that made our Lord cry, "Father, if it be possible, let this cup pass from me." But, thank God, He finally cried, "Not my will, but thine, be done!"

> Out of the woods my Master went,
> And He was well content.
> Out of the woods my Master came,
> Content with death and shame.
>
> When Death and Shame would woo Him last,
> From under the trees they drew Him last:
> 'Twas on a tree they slew Him—last
> When out of the woods He came.

SECTION III
The Precious Blood of Christ

For the law having a shadow of good things to come, and not the very image of the things, can never with those sacrifices which they offered year by year continually make the comers thereunto perfect. For then would they not have ceased to be offered? because that the worshippers once purged should have had no more conscience of sins. But in those sacrifices there is a remembrance again made of sins every year. For it is not possible that the blood of bulls and of goats should take away sins. Wherefore when he cometh into the world, he saith, Sacrifice and offering thou wouldest not, but a body hast thou prepared me: in burnt offerings and sacrifices for sin thou hast had no pleasure. Then said I, Lo, I come (in the volume of the book it is written of me,) to do thy will, O God. Above when he said, Sacrifice and offering and burnt offering and offering for sin thou wouldest not, neither hadst pleasure therein; which are offered by the law; then said he, Lo, I come to do thy will, O God. He taketh away the first, that he may establish the second.

HEBREWS 10:1-9

Section III: The Precious Blood of Christ

"THERE IS POWER IN THE BLOOD OF THE LAMB"

The ninth chapter of Hebrews tells us over and over again that everything connected with the Tabernacle and its services was a shadow of the "greater and more perfect tabernacle, not made with hands," that is, the Lord Jesus Christ. The ninth chapter of this epistle also calls the Tabernacle a pattern "of things in the heavens" and goes so far as to say, "It was therefore necessary that the *patterns* of things in the heavens should be purified with these [the blood of animals]; but the heavenly things themselves with better sacrifices than these. For Christ is not entered into the holy places made with hands, which are the *figures* of the true; but into heaven itself, now to appear in the presence of God for us: nor yet that he should offer himself often, as the high priest entereth into the holy place every year with blood of others; for then must he often have suffered since the foundation of the world: but now once in the end of the world hath he appeared to put away sin by the sacrifice of himself."

We see again the precious blood that flows from the beginning of the Bible to the very end.

"POWER"

If fallen man trifles with atomic power, he will find that sooner or later, perhaps much sooner than he thinks, it will bring him to disaster. The scientists are talking glibly about "harnessing" this power which is in the atom. Dynamite has a hundred times the explosive power of gunpowder, and TNT has a hundred times the power of nitroglycerine, but one pound of uranium has thirty million times the power of TNT. Scientists are talking about harnessing this atomic energy, but they might as well talk about harnessing the devil. They might as well talk about harnessing thirty million demons. Fallen man is not going to tell atomic energy where to go. Atomic energy is going to tell fallen man where to go, and fallen man will go there amazingly soon unless he gets on his knees and repents and cries to God.

The Prophet Daniel says in the twelfth chapter (verse 4) of his prophecy: "But thou, O Daniel, shut up the words, and seal the book, even to the time of the end."

I believe we are living in the time of the end. Men are running to and fro, in this age of grace, but they are not running to and fro with the Gospel. Knowledge is increasing, but not wisdom, and not truth.

We must find a way of protection from the atomic bomb. Can anybody show a way other than Christ? Can we have peace on this earth without good will toward men? Can we have peace without the Prince of Peace?

There is a way to protect us from atomic energy. Jesus Christ is, of course, the Way, the Truth and the Life. But this world has clearly said, "We will not have this man to reign over us," and the Bible just as clearly declares, "He that hath the Son hath life; and he that hath not the Son of God hath not life." This world does not want the Way. It does not want the Truth, and it is definitely turning its back on Life. The world will have to accept the alternative—which is death.

Yes, there is power in atoms—in atomic energy. But there is more power in a single drop of the blood of the Lord Jesus Christ than in all the atoms in the universe! As long as this age lasts, it is your privilege and mine to tell the good news that the blood of Jesus Christ, God's Son, cleanses us from all sin.

THE SEED OF THE WOMAN
SHALL BRUISE THE SERPENT'S HEAD

This message of the blood that runs like a scarlet thread through the entire Bible begins in Genesis 3:15, where God made the first promise of the Redeemer. Sin had come into the world, and God pronounced the doom of Satan and at the same time held up the hope of the coming seed of the woman. God declared that the seed of the woman would bruise the serpent's head, and the serpent would bruise His heal.

This is the embryo and the germ of all Messianic Prophecy. Notice that the doom of Satan will be accomplished by the seed of the woman. Observe that it does not mention *the seed of the man,* even though among Orientals men are given prominence and women are in the background. It does not speak of *the seed of the man and the woman.* But the verse speaks simply of *the seed of the woman.* In the fullness of time the Lord Jesus was born of the Virgin Mary. Furthermore, this verse says that Satan, or the serpent, will bruise the heel of the coming Messiah. When you execute a man by hanging, you do not bruise his heel. When you execute a man by beheading him, you do not bruise his heel; neither do you bruise his heel by stoning or piercing him; but when you hammer nails through a man's tender feet, you bruise his heel!

God dramatized this abstract prophecy about the coming Redeemer, and immediately made for Adam and his wife "coats of skins, and clothed them" (Genesis 3:21).

I would stake my faith in the Bible and in Christianity on that one verse alone. Sin had come into the world and the first sinners were hiding in utter fear and terror. God came to seek and to save that which was lost. God made for Adam and his wife coats of skin and clothed them. How are coats of skin obtained? An animal had to die. I believe that in this instance also it was a lamb, and without spot and without blemish. Its blood had to be shed. It had to become naked so that Adam and Eve could be clothed. It had to die for them, and then its beautiful clean coat was put around them, to make them fit to appear in the presence of a holy God. In other words, we have here (1) the complete philosophy of the Atonement, (2) the principle of vicarious suffering, and (3) the eternal principle that without the shedding of blood there is no remission of sin. Christ had to die so I could live. Christ had to shed His blood to save me. Christ had to become naked so I could become clothed, and now I stand before God not clothed in my own righteousness, which is as filthy rags, but in "that which is through the faith of Christ, the righteousness which is of God by faith."

Furthermore, we have in this incident the elements of all the so-called "comparative religions." In order to make themselves fit to appear in the presence of God, sinful Adam and Eve finally attempted to dress themselves in fig leaves, and we find every false religion from Cain and Abel to the present wrapped somewhere in those fig leaves. All so-called "religions" are man's vain attempt to climb to a holy God. The Gospel is God's glorious condescension, His coming all the way down to sinful man.

"THE LORD HAD RESPECT UNTO ABEL AND TO HIS OFFERING"

Adam and Eve had children. Two prominent ones were Cain and Abel. They were told that the blood of sacrifice was their only approach to a holy God, but they had to decide for themselves what sacrifice they would present. One crucial day the time for the decision came. Cain utterly ignored the revelation of God, and instead of bringing a spotless little lamb, he brought the fruits of the ground and trees that he had developed with what he considered great scientific and horticultural skill. But Abel came and laid a bleeding little lamb on the altar of God.

I can see haughty Cain standing stiff-necked in front of his pretentious altar piled high with fruits.

At the other altar kneels humble, believing Abel, while before him lies the bleeding little lamb. "And God the Lord had respect unto Abel and to his offering: but unto Cain and to his offering he had not respect."

Now God begins to exhort sinful Cain. The boys are on the way back to the field. The heart of Abel is filled with joy and peace. Abel is redeemed and knows it. The heart of Cain is full of hell and wickedness. But God gives him another chance, as He may, at this particular moment and in the closing days of this age, be giving you. He cries, "Cain, Why art thou wroth? and why is thy countenance fallen? If thou doest well, shalt thou not be accepted?" Here God means not only that Cain's countenance could be lifted up, but the Hebrew indicates that the offering of the lamb should be lifted up. Then He adds, "And if thou doest not well, sin lieth at the door . . . and do thou rule over it."

In other words, God says, "If you won't come by way of the blood of the lamb, then you'll have to rule over sin yourself, and you'll have to go your own way."

That is exactly what God is saying today to the entire world. We hear that the world stands at the crossroads, since atomic energy has been discovered. But that is not true. The world is not standing at the crossroads. The world is standing on the brink of hell, and at any moment it may go over. God came to seek and to save that which was lost. He is exhorting us once more, "If thou doest well, shalt it not be lifted up? and if thou doest not well, sin lieth at the door . . . and do thou rule over it," in other words, "That great fact of sin, and of life, and of judgment, and of eternity—if you won't let Me handle it for you, then you will have to handle it yourself."

But Cain would not take God's way any more than man will take God's way today, and you know only too well how Cain handled the problem of sin and eternity.

While Abel sang for joy, Cain became more and more enraged until finally he picked up a rock and murdered his own brother, and his brother's blood cried to God from the ground.

"BUT UNTO CAIN AND TO HIS OFFERING HE HAD NOT RESPECT"

Life, God and eternity are serious realities. When Jesus Christ said, "I am the way, the truth, and the life," He meant it in the absolute sense. There is no way for this life or the life to come other than Christ. There is no truth in this world or in the world to come other than Christ. The life for you now and for all eternity is Christ. "He that hath the Son hath life; and he that hath not the Son of God hath not life," but "the wrath of God abideth on him."

Cain did not want the Lamb of God, "which taketh away the sin of the world." This world apparently does not want Him, either. There was no place for Him to lay His head when He was in this world. There was a stable for Him to be born in, but no room in the inn. There was no bed for Him to die on, but He was hung between earth and heaven in a vertical position on the Cross, as if He were not fit for heaven, so held down by nails, and not fit for earth, so "lifted up from the earth on a cross." He was pushed out of this world by the point of a Roman spear, and after two thousand years Europe and Asia and even England and America are saying, in effect, "We will not have this man to rule over us."

If the world does not choose life, it has no alternative but death. If it does not choose the Light of the World, it has no alternative but blackouts. If it does not choose the Prince of Peace, it has no alternative but wars and desolations to the end. The world has cried, "Not this man, but Barabbas; give us Barabbas!"

On the day the first atomic bomb was unleashed, President Truman and the scientists made two statements: first, "We have discovered a monster that can destroy the human race"; second "We must immediately find a way to harness this monster."

The first statement is true; the second is hopeless.

If any of you are like Cain, who had a second opportunity as you have now—a second and maybe a last opportunity— accept Jesus Christ and lift up the offering that God wants, namely, "the Lamb slain from the foundation of the world." "The Lord had respect unto Abel and to his offering: but unto Cain and to his offering he had not respect."

It is a profoundly moving experience to listen as God gives Cain a second opportunity and begs him to lift up the offering before it is too late. It is not God's will that any should perish. God is infinite love, and at the same time God is absolutely holy. The very first attribute of God is not His love but His holiness. God wanted to receive Cain, but God could not! God could not unless Cain would come by the way of the Cross.

Why do I dare say that God "could not"? I say so because the Bible reveals that. I say so because even God's own Son, in the Garden of Gethsemane, with strong crying and tears, begged His Father, "If it be possible, let this cup pass from me." But it was not possible, even for Omnipotence. It was not possible even for Almighty God to forgive you and me apart from the precious blood of Jesus Christ.

"HOLY, HOLY, HOLY"

Over and above all things, God is holy. In the Wilderness Tabernacle He dwelt directly over the Mercy Seat on the Golden Ark of the Covenant, between the heads of the cherubim in the Holy of Holies. That is why no human being could dare to enter the Holy of Holies. That is why God permitted the high priest to come in on only one day of the year, and then "not without blood, which he offered for himself, and for the errors of the people: the Holy Ghost this signifying, that the way into the holiest of all was not yet made manifest, while as the first tabernacle was yet stand-ing . . . Which stood only in meats and drinks, and divers washing . . . imposed on them until the time of reformation. But Christ being come an high priest of good things to come, by a greater and more perfect tabernacle, not made with hands, that is to say, not of this building; neither by the blood of goats and calves, but by his own blood he entered in once into the holy place, having obtained eternal redemption for us."

When you begin to understand the utter holiness of God, you will marvel at the precious blood of Christ typified so gloriously in all these ancient Hebrew sacrifices. God is utterly holy, and because He is holy, I must emphasize that it is impossible for Him to allow you to approach Him apart from the blood of Christ.

Notice that there were kneeling, or lying prostrate, on the Ark in the Holy of Holies two cherubim. We picture these as sweet angels, but they were terrible beings. They have one duty to perform through time and eternity: they guard the holiness of God. They are not angels; they are not archangels or seraphim; they are cherubim. They have one duty, and only one duty. They guard the holiness of God. The sword of vengeance would have to fall on the high priest should he so much as dare to step into the Holy of Holies without blood.

Josephus, the historian of the first century, gives an ex-tensive description, similar to that in Scripture, of this Wilder-ness Tabernacle. He declares that the high priest had a silken cord attached to his ankle so that should he for any reason not take the blood into the Holy of Holies with him the other priests could pull him out by the cord. But this would be impossible. His coming into the Holy of Holies without the blood would have produced a result more violent than an explosion of all the atomic energy in the universe. Sin and holiness cannot be together.

Apparently it is the duty of the cherubim to prevent this

and to guard the holiness of God. The angels—the arch-angels, the seraphim and all the others—have duties to perform, but throughout the Bible the cherubim are spoken of as being used by God to guard His own holiness. Notice that when sin first came into the world, it was not angels, or archangels, but cherubim, with terrible flaming swords turning in every direction, that guarded the entrance to the tree of life.

God wants to receive everyone, but He cannot apart from the blood of the everlasting covenant. God wanted to receive Cain, and He wants to receive you, no matter how wicked you are. It is not God's will that any should perish. But God is holy.

In the dark days of the Civil War a young Lieutenant learned that his wife in New England was dying. The young officer was stationed on the southern shores of the Potomac, just opposite the White House. He begged General McClellan for a two-week furlough, but the general said it was impossible to give him more than a twenty-four-hour leave, and that no one in the entire army could extend the leave. "No one," said McClellan, "but the Commander in Chief, Abraham Lincoln. If you could get face to face with him, he would give you your furlough, but it is impossible to get near him these days. Even colonels," said the general, "have to stand in line for days, and a lieutenant could never make it."

However, the lieutenant took the twenty-four-hour pass in the solemn hope that somehow and some way he could come face to face with the man who lived in the White House. He rowed across the Potomac but was halted by a sentry. A second attempt was also unsuccessful. He gave up in despair and let his boat drift. It floated into a little cove where a boy was fishing. The little fellow heard the lieutenant sobbing and voluteered to help him. The officer unburdened his heart to the lad and the boy concluded, "So all you want to do is to just see the President, and just come near enough so you can talk with him?" The little fellow saluted and said, "Lieutenant, I can help you."

The officer did not know what to believe, and he did not care to look for an explanation. As he went through the forest with his hand in the hand of the little boy, he saw only one thing: he was coming closer and closer to the White House.

When they reached an open road, the lieutenant's heart failed him when he saw a sentry, six feet tall and with a gleaming bayonet. But when the guard saw the couple he did not challenge them: he merely clicked his heels, presented arms, and winked at the little boy. The lieutenant did not understand. But he knew he was getting closer and closer to the White House.

At last they reached it, and standing in front of the steps leading to the White House were two more sentries, who seemed taller than the first one the lieutenant had seen, and whose bayonets seemed to gleam more terribly in the sunlight. But these two, standing like statues, offered no challenge. They clicked their heels again, presented arms, and once more the lieutenant thought he saw them wink. Up the steps marched the officer and the boy, past two more sentries at the door of the White House. Then they hurried down the corridor, past two more sentries, and with no ceremony whatsoever the little lad rushed to the door of Abraham Lincoln's room and almost pulled the surprised lieutenant in after him. The Great Emancipator looked down at his son (of course it was Tad Lincoln) and with a laugh he asked, "Tad, Tad, whom do you have there? What do you mean by bursting into my office like this?" With one hand Tad Lincoln held the hand of his father, and with the other hand he held that of the surprised lieutenant. And of course you know the rest of the story.

The great and holy God dwells in the Holy of Holies. Your sins have separated you from Him. But in the mystery of the Atonement, Jesus Christ came here, and with one pierced hand He holds the hand of His Father, and with the other pierced hand He holds yours.

So the precious blood of Christ flows on through the Old Testament. The points we have cited about the lamb were specified by God Himself in regard to the Passover lamb, which typified the Lord Jesus Christ, who beautifully fulfilled every specification and feature, so that the inspired writer calls Jesus Christ "our passover . . . sacrificed for us."

The "Greater and More Perfect Tabernacle, Not Made with Hands"

And after the Passover came the Wilderness Tabernacle. Now no man can doubt that Christ is the "greater and more perfect tabernacle, not made with hands." The Tabernacle forshadowed Jesus Christ in every detail. In general it foreshadowed the tabernacle of the body in which Christ dwelt. In particular, every piece of furniture in the Tabernacle, such as the Golden Candlestick, and the Golden Table of Shewbread, and the other equipment, foreshadowed the Lord Jesus as the Light of the World and the Bread of Life.

As we have mentioned, even the colors used in the Tabernacle foreshadowed the Lord Jesus. The colors were blue, purple, scarlet, and white fine-twined linen. They were not chosen by God arbitrarily. He had a purpose in selecting these colors, just as He had in everything connected with the Wilderness Tabernacle. God selected blue because the greater and more perfect Tabernacle, Jesus Christ, was of heavenly origin. "Ye are from beneath," said the Lord Jesus. "I am from above." God selected purple because His Son was King of kings and Lord of lords. Purple is the color of royalty. When the King came the first time for us He was crowned with thorns and came as the Lamb of God "which taketh away the sin of the world." But when He comes the second time He will not wear a crown of thorns, but the diadem of the universe. Then the kingdoms of this world shall become the kingdoms of our Lord and He shall reign for ever and ever, hallelujah! When He came the first time there was no room for Him in the inn, and not even the innkeeper of Bethlehem stood outside the door with a lantern to welcome the King of kings. But when He comes the second time every eye shall see Him, and every knee shall bow, and every tongue shall confess that Jesus Christ is Lord, to the glory of God the Father.

God selected scarlet because of the blood that begins to flow in Genesis and flows throughout the Bible until we come to the blessed Cross of Calvary, where there is a fountain filled with blood drawn from Immanuel's veins. God selected white fine-twined linen because of the wondrous spotlessness of the human character of Jesus Christ. How eloquent the language of the Tabernacle!

SECTION IV
Our High Priest

Now of the things which we have spoken this is the sum: We have such an high priest, who is set on the right hand of the throne of the Majesty in the heavens; a minister of the sanctuary, and of the true tabernacle, which the Lord pitched, and not man. For every high priest is ordained to offer gifts and sacrifices: wherefore it is of necessity that this man have somewhat also to offer.   —HEBREWS 8:1-3

It was therefore necessary that the patterns of things in the heavens should be purified with these; but the heavenly things themselves with better sacrifices than these. For Christ is not entered into the holy places made with hands, which are the figures of the true; but into heaven itself, now to appear in the presence of God for us: nor yet that he should offer himself often, as the high priest entereth into the holy place every year with blood of others; for then must he often have suffered since the foundation of the world: but now once in the end of the world hath he appeared to put away sin by the sacrifice of himself. And as it it appointed unto men once to die, but after this the judgment: so Christ was once offered to bear the sins of many; and unto them that look for him shall he appear the second time without sin unto salvation.
—HEBREWS 9:23-28

Section IV: Our High Priest

Jesus Christ was definitely foreshadowed by the high priest of the ancient Tabernacle. It was the high priest who carried the blood into the Holy of Holies. This great symbolic service was performed only once in the entire year. "Now of the things which we have spoken this is the sum: We have such an high priest, who is set on the right hand of the throne of the Majesty in the heavens; a minister of the sanctuary, and of the true tabernacle, which the Lord pitched, and not man. For every high priest is ordained to offer gifts and sacrifices: wherefore it is of necessity that this man have somewhat also to offer" (Hebrews 8:1-3). "It was therefore necessary that the *patterns* of things in the heavens should be purified with these; but the heavenly things themselves with better sacrifices than these. For Christ is not entered into the holy places made with hands, which are the *figures* of the true; but into heaven itself, now to appear in the presence of God for us: nor yet that he should offer himself often, as the high priest entereth into the holy place every year with blood of other; for then must he often have suffered since the foundation of the world: but now once in the end of the world hath he appeared to put away sin by the sacrifice of himself" (Hebrews 9:23-26).

The directions that God gives in Exodus and Leviticus regarding the garments of the high priest indicate that when he went into the Holy of Holies on the Day of Atonement he must wear plain white garments. Only the faithful could believe that the high priest had gone into the Holy of Holies, and that he was performing the service for them. The cynic and the skeptic did not accept his work by faith because they belonged to the group who say, "We believe only that which we can see."

The high priest had gone from sight but God had a way for the faithful. God still has a way for the faithful, and our High Priest is now in the presence of God for us. On the bottom of the white robe of the high priest was a series of golden bells and pomegranates, and these beautiful bells made a tinkling sound, for those who had ears to hear.

Do you doubt that our High Priest is in the presence of God now, in the eternal Holy of Holies? Are you one of those who believe only what they see? Or have you heard the tinkling of the golden bells? It is a blessed experience to send a prayer to our High Priest and then listen for the tinkling of a little bell and hear it ring plainly when the answer comes back! It is a soul-stirring experience for us to recognize direct guidance from God and the specific leading of Divine Providence. When you have such an experience do you not hear a little golden bell ring? And are you not perfectly content to believe, even though you cannot see, that our High Priest has entered "into heaven itself, now to appear in the presence of God for us"?

"And unto Them That Look for Him Shall He Appear the Second Time"

The Wilderness Tabernacle not only symbolized and foreshadowed the first advent of the blessed Christ: it also foreshadowed His second advent, for the high priest came out of the Holy of Holies of the Wilderness Tabernacle and appeared to the people a second time, and this time He wore a most gorgeous and beautiful garment, described in Exodus. He perhaps tarried in the Holy Place and abandoned his white robe and assumed the gorgeous attire in which he appeared unto the people a *second* time. "So Christ was once offered to bear the sins of many; and unto them that look for Him

shall He appear the second time without sin unto salvation"
(Hebrews 9:28).

"THE LIFE OF THE FLESH IS IN THE BLOOD"

As you stand in the Holy Place and gaze at the glittering
wonders, does not this thought strike you, "How much God
must love us!"? But the most precious type of all is the blood,
the wonderful blood. We are dealing with a mystery when
we speak of blood. However, the Bible is always specific and
scientific, no matter what subject it discusses. Scripture was
3,500 years ahead of the scientist when it declared (Leviticus
17:11), "For the life of the flesh is in the blood: and I
have given it to you upon the altar to make an atonement
for your souls: for it is the blood that maketh an atonement
for the soul."

Science now declares it to be a fact that the life of an
organism is in the blood. But science did not know that a
hundred years ago. In fact, a hundred years ago science
did not even know that the blood circulated! Until Dr.
Harvey's time no one dreamed of the circulation of blood
in the human body. But God knew.

Not even in eternity will we know *how* the blood of Jesus
Christ God's Son cleanses us from all sin. But thank God
we can know for time and eternity *that* the blood of Jesus
Christ, God's Son cleanses us from all sin!

Louis Pasteur's co-worker in the demonstration of what
used to be called the "germ theory" was Dr. Felix Ruh, a
Jewish doctor in Paris. Ruh demonstrated the use of antitoxin
for diphtheria in the following amazing way. The physician's
granddaughter died of black diphtheria, and Dr. Ruh, vowing
that he would find out what killed his granddaughter, locked
himself in his laboratory for days. He emerged with a fierce
determination to prove, with his colleague Louis Pasteur,
that the "germ theory" was more than a theory.

The famous Pasteur had been exiled by Emperor Louis of

France. The Medical Association had disapproved of Pasteur and had succeeded in getting him exiled, but he did not go far from Paris. He hid in the forest and erected a laboratory in which to continue his forbidden research.

It was a great moment in history when Felix Ruh joined his exiled colleague and together they worked out the germ theory. Dr. Ruh directed the climax experiment in the obtaining of antitoxin for black diphtheria.

Twenty beautiful horses were led out into the forest to the improvised laboratory. Scientists, doctors and nurses came to watch the experiment. Ruh opened a steel vault and took out a large pail filled with black diphtheria germs, which he had cultured carefully for four months. There were enough germs in that pail to kill everybody in France. The scientist went to each beautiful horse and swabbed its nostrils, tongue, throat and eyes with these deadly germs.

The scientists waited several days to see the outcome. Every horse except one developed a terrific fever, rolled over and died. Most of the doctors and scientists wearied of the experiment and did not remain for what they thought to be the death of the last horse.

For several more days this final horse lingered, lying pathetically on the ground with his eyes rolled back. The orderlys on duty while Ruh, Pasteur and several others were sleeping on cots in the stables had been instructed to awaken the scientist should there be any change in the animal's temperature.

About two A.M. the temperature showed a half-degree decrease, and the orderly awakened the scientist. By morning the thermometer had dropped two more degrees, and by night the fever was gone entirely and the horse was able to stand, eat and drink.

Then Dr. Ruh took a sledge hammer and struck that beautiful horse a deathblow between the eyes. The scientists drew all the blood from the veins of this animal which had developed the disease but had overcome it. The scientists were driven posthaste to the Municipal Hospital in Paris. They bludgeoned their way past the superintendent and guards and forced an entrance into a ward where three hundred babies had been segregated to die from black diphtheria. With the blood of the horse they forcibly inoculated every one of these babies. All but three lived and recovered completely. They were saved by the blood of an overcomer.

As these babies were saved by the blood of an overcomer, so we are saved by the blood of an overcomer. The horse had the terrible disease and was able to overcome it, and his blood enabled the babies to overcome the disease also. So Christ, "who knew no sin, was made sin for us." and we, too, are saved by the blood of an overcomer.

"I Have Given It to You upon the Altar to Make an Atonement for Your Souls"

The Brazen Altar of Sacrifice stood at the very foot of the cross formed by the arrangement of the furniture in the Wilderness Tabernacle. Of course, the Brazen Altar was a type of Christ, our Sacrifice. Brass was the symbol of judgment, as in the case of the Brazen Serpent of the Wilderness and the Brazen Laver that stood at the door of the Wilderness Tabernacle.

At the Brazen Altar of Sacrifice the judgment fell upon the spotless Lamb of God, but where there was judgment there was at once mercy because the Lamb suffered for the sinner. Christ suffered for us and took the judgment we deserved. The Brazen Laver at the door of the Tabernacle also spoke of judgment, because, made of the women's looking glasses, it reflected the sinner and showed him it was impossible for him to enter as he was into the Holy Place of God. But again we see mercy symbolized, because in the Brazen Laver was the cleansing water, and immediately with the judgment there was also the provision to wash the sinner from his sins. The Brazen Laver was, therefore, a type of Jesus Christ and His cleansing power.

In the serpent of brass, which was lifted on a pole in the Wilderness, we see God's terrible judgment of sin. But we see with the judgment the infinite mercy of God.

Christ *became* sin for us! The spotless and holy Lamb of God became something like that judged serpent hanging on that pole. Incidentally, the pole must have had a cross-piece at the top, because a metal serpent could not be hung upon a bare pole. The banner poles of the Israelites had such a crosspiece. Whosoever looked was healed! "And as Moses lifted up the serpent in the wilderness, even so must the Son of man be lifted up: that whosoever believeth in him should not perish, but have eternal life" (John 3:14-15).

By comparing Exodus 25:10 with Exodus 27:1 you will find that the Brazen Altar of Sacrifice was twice the height of the Mercy Seat in the Holy of Holies. We see that the Atonement does something more than save sinners—it glorifies God (John 17:4). It was on the Brazen Altar of Sacrifice that the animals were killed and offered up whole as an offering to God. There was a horn on each corner of the altar. Horns are always the symbol of power, and the horns on the altar pointed to every corner of the universe—north, south, east and west—suggesting that the power of the atonement of Christ is infinite and that we have but to trust in Him and fling ourselves upon the mercy of God.

Duplicates of this altar were made and placed by God's direction in several Cities of Refuge throughout the Holy Land, and any miserable fellow who was pursued by his enemies but reached one of these Cities of Refuge and managed to get hold of the horns of the altar could not be touched by any law. Even if he were chased by every Jewish lawyer and constable and bill collector in Palestine, so long as he had hold of the altar he was safe.

The atonement of Christ and His blessed Cross makes us secure, and the blood on the altar makes us safe from all the devils and demons in hell, and we can cry with Paul, "I am persuaded, that neither death, nor life, nor angels, nor principalities, nor powers, nor things present, nor things to come, nor height, nor depth, nor any other creature, shall be able to separate us from the love of God, which is in Christ Jesus our Lord" (Romans 8:38-39).

From the Holy of Holies to the Brazen Altar

This altar, however, was bloody. It was a scene of continuous agony and slaughter and blood. It was at the extreme distance from the Holy of Holies, a fact which symbolized the distance that God Almighty traveled from heaven to Calvary to save your soul.

In the Holy of Holies everything was calm and peaceful and serene and beutiful, in wonderful contrast to the scene at the bloody altar. But—

> Out of the ivory palaces
> Into a world of woe,
> Only His great eternal love
> Made my Saviour go.

The footsteps of God Almighty, from the highest heights in heaven to the lowest place on earth, are marked by infinite love, and, the footprints all the way back from the Brazen Altar of Sacrifice into the Holy of Holies of heaven are marked by blood. We have but to follow the blood-stained path to find ourselves at last in the presence of God.

Are you beginning to comprehend the height, the length, the breadth, and the depth of the love of God in Christ Jesus our Lord? We will need all eternity to understand just one adverb in the Bible, and that adverb is the two-letter word *so* (John 3:16).

No wonder that throughout the Old Testament the great Creator foreshadowed the precious blood. No wonder that the fallen human race had to be given types, shadows, pictures, symbols and object lessons. Words would never be enough to tell this story. Words are adequate for the isms and spasms of our day, but not for the blessed Gospel of Christ. The Gospel is not words but *the Word*. Thank God that after centuries of types and symbols "the Word was made flesh, and dwelt among us."

SECTION V
It Is All Godlike

For when Moses had spoken every precept to all the people according to the law, he took the blood of calves and of goats, with water, and scarlet wool, and hyssop, and sprinkled both the book, and all the people, saying, This is the blood of the testament which God hath enjoined unto you. Moreover he sprinkled with blood both the tabernacle, and all the vessels of the ministry. And almost all things are by the law purged with blood; and without shedding of blood is no remission.
—HEBREWS 9:19-22

And from Jesus Christ, who is the faithful witness, and the first begotten of the dead, and the prince of the kings of the earth. Unto him that loved us, and washed us from our sins in his own blood, and hath made us kings and priests unto God and his Father; to him be glory and dominion for ever and ever. Amen.
—REVELATION 1:5-6

Section V: It Is All Godlike

The Gospel is Godlike. It is Godlike in kind (Romans 3:21). It is the righteousness of God which we receive, not righteousness that we could manufacture, but the righteousness which He Himself *is*. The blood of Christ does not restore us to the original status of innocence which Adam and Eve had before the fall. It does infinitely more that that. The blood of Christ does not merely make us what we might have been before the fall. We are actually made kings and priests unto God, heirs and joint-heirs with Christ! First John 3:2 declares, "It doth not yet appear what we shall be: but we know that, when he shall appear, we shall be like him; for we shall see him as he is." In Revelation 1:5-6 we read, "Unto him that loved us, and washed us from our sins in his own blood, and hath made us kings and priests unto God and his Father; to him be the glory and dominion for ever and ever. Amen."

Furthermore, the blessed Gospel is Godlike in *length.* By the grace of God we are given eternal life, not merely life from now on, but life that never began and will never end. Whether we can understand it or not, it is Godlike, without beginning or ending.

Salvation is Godlike in *thoroughness.* "As far as the east is from the west, so far hath he removed our transgressions from us."

No wonder theologians have never been able to make a "theory" of the Atonement! "My thoughts are not your thoughts, neither are my ways your ways . . . . For as the heavens are higher than the earth, so are my ways higher than your ways, and my thoughts than your thoughts." Theologians have tried in vain to "explain" the Atonement: It is a mystery understood only by the Creator: Only God knows what went on during those three hours of darkness on Golgotha. In some way the Creator was creating eternal life for doomed, lost sinners.

When it comes to explaining life of any kind or prying into the secret of life with microscope, telescope, or test tube—well, that is just a bit over the professors' heads.

The definitions of the word "life" in the biology books and dictionaries are almost humorous in their inadequacy. But the authors of the definitions seem to be blissfully ignorant of the fact that they have not defined the term!

The popular definition of life is this: Life is existence between birth and death. This definition tells the duration of life or what someone thinks is life's duration but it does not give even a suggestion of what life is.

Vegetable life, animal life, any kind of life, is beyond the reach of our senses. You cannot smell life, see life, feel life, hear life, or taste life, in its essence. What is a rose seed? When you plant a rose seed do you really know what happens? Do you know the *modus operandi?* Do you—or does anyone—know what takes place when a rose seed is transformed into glorious roses on a rose bush?

Since God guards so carefully the secrets of life in the vegetable world, one can see that the Creator will guard even more closely His secret of eternal life. Do not try to make a "theory" of the Atonement. Fall on your knees before the sacred Cross and weep your heart out in tears of gratitude.

No, you cannot, and perhaps never will, see behind the scenes of Calvary. You can hear weeping and crying and screaming. You may even hear the rattling of the dice in the helmets of the soldiers as they gambled for the seamless cloak of the blessed Christ. You may hear the sharp orders of the centurion, the hissing and the howling of the scribes and the Pharisees. You may hear the thunder and feel the earthquake. You may even hear the cry of the Victor when He declares, "It is finished." But behind the scenes you can never go. Only God has that sacred priviledge.

The glorious salvation in Christ is Godlike also in its *cost.* I would not leave the city of gold to walk the dusty road of Calvary. I would not exchange the diadem of the universe for a crown of thorns. I would not leave the songs and the praises of angels and seraphim for the howling and the hissing of the scribes and the Pharisees. I would not stretch out my arms to a lost world if my hands had to be held in place by Roman nails. I would not have a way opened back to my heart if it had to be opened by the point of a Roman spear. I would not do that. But God would, and God *did!* The Gospel is Godlike in cost.

Finally, the Gospel is Godlike in *presentation.* It is a gift. If it were wages that we received, the Gospel would be businesslike, not Godlike. It is utter nonsense for anybody to imagine he can buy a few billion years with anything that he could possibly do in threescore years and ten.

There are only four ways in which anything can be acquired. You can acquire a thing, if it can be acquired at all, (1) by honestly earning it; (2) by dishonestly stealing it; (3) by buying it; (4) by receiving it as a gift.

There is nothing you can do to earn eternal life. You certainly cannot steal it, and as for buying it, you do not have the price. There is only One who had the price, and He paid it fully for us.

That leaves the only other possible way to acquire anything —by gift—and thank God "the gift of God is eternal life."

"Please, Your Royal Highness," said a scrubwoman to a princess in the conservatory of a king, "please, I like to buy just one bunch of those purple grapes. The doctors say my sick little boy must have those purple grapes. Please, I like to buy. Ask your father. Tell him I like to buy."

The princess went to the grapevine, and with her silver scissors she cut not one, or two, or three, or four bunches of the purple grapes, but all the scrubwoman could possibly carry in her apron. Said the princess with justified scorn, "Buy the grapes from my father? *Buy* them! My father is not a merchant who sells. My father is a king, and he *gives.*" Salvation is Godlike in its presentation.

I am glad salvation is a gift, because there is something romantic about a gift. There is nothing romantic about earning wages, and God, of course, is love itself.

Suppose that December 15 is your wife's birthday. Suppose, further, that on the night of the fourteenth she reminds you that the next day is the fifteenth, and you keep on reading the paper and pay no attention to her remark. But then she repeats the statement and declares that the next day is her birthday. Suppose you pay no attention whatsoever but continue to read the newspaper or listen to the radio. But your wife mentions what she has done for you and says, "Well, it is my birthday tomorrow. What am I going to get for doing all the things I've done?"

So you yawn (of course, this is pure supposition!), reach for your checkbook, write out a check, toss it to her, and say "All right, here's your wages for this year. Don't let me hear anything more about it."

Is that money a gift? Or is it wages? Now, suppose that when December 15 comes you cannot give your wife that birthday present you want to give her, as you have only ninety cents. But you get her a box of her favorite candy and the morning of her birthday you say lovingly, "Happy birthday." What is the box of candy? It is not wages. It is a gift.

"How Much Did It Cost?"

The first thing many want to know about a gift is: How much did it cost? This inquisitiveness is so general that the large department stores in New York City employ extra price clerks for a week after Christmas so that curious women can find out the exact cost of the Christmas presents they received.

Ask God Almighty how much the gift of eternal life cost! Ask the angels who look down from the battlements of heaven. Ask the Virgin Mary as she stands beneath the Cross with hot salty tears streaming from her eyes. Ask the Great God as with His own strong arm he holds back the legions of angels. Ask the blessed Christ as He cries in the darkness, "My God, my God, why hast thou forsaken me?"

While I was still in seminary I served a church in Beemerville, New Jersey. You will find in that building, according to the company which installed them, the most beautiful church windows this firm has placed in any rural church in the entire state. But to the right of the preacher is a window that was never installed.

James Jarvey, the multimillionaire, lived in the town, and he promised me a thousand dollars for that window, for which I was to select the design. Jarvey than left for Europe.

The dedication service for the windows was delayed until this "climax window" was installed. One day a young city salesman came to the parsonage on a mission—to change my choice of the design for the thousand-dollar window. I had selected Hoffman's *Golgotha* because it meant so much to me and because I wanted everyone who came into the church to have that wonderful masterpiece continually before his eyes.

But the young salesman finally had to be brutally frank because I would not change my mind. He tried to point out that *Golgotha* would be "anticlimactic" and "nonaesthetic." He described the beauty of one window which depicted green fields and running brooks, and another which showed the mountains of the Holy Land, and another which portrayed the Good Shepherd, and then he said, "Don't you see, Reverend, this *Golgotha* thing would spoil it all. The picture is gruesome and bloody and smacks of the slaughterhouse."

I did not let him comment further, and his window was never installed.

I am going to tell you something about the Wilderness Tabernacle, something which some people have told me not to emphasize. But as long as I live I will emphasize it. The beautiful Wilderness Tabernacle, with its golden walls, its golden furniture and its magnificent blue, purple, scarlet, and white fine-twined linen, *was covered with blood*!

"For when Moses had spoken every precept to all the people according to the law, he took the blood of calves and of goats, with water, and scarlet wool, and hyssop, and sprinkled both the book, and all the people, saying, This is the blood of the testament which God hath enjoined unto you. Moreover he sprinkled with blood both *the tabernacle, and all the vessels of the ministry.* And almost all things are by the law purged with blood; and without shedding of blood is no remission" (Hebrews 9:19-22).

Have I ruined your picture of the beautiful golden-walled Tabernacle? Or have I made it more beautiful because now it becomes a perfect type of the Lord Jesus Christ! "His visage was so marred more than any man, and his form more than the sons of men."

When my mother lay in her casket in Newark, New Jersey, twenty years ago, we children went upstairs during the long night to look at some of her belongings. Among other things, we found a photograph of her when she was a young girl of twenty, skating in the park. She was lovely. But when we came downstairs to see her as she lay in her last sleep, we remarked, "She is more beautiful now." Her hair had turned white, her forehead was wrinkled, and care lines were showing in her face.

But some of those gray hairs we had put there. Some of these lines we had engraved there. And they showed the price she paid for us.

When Martin Luther was a monk in a monastery, he knelt on the stone floor, held the crucifix before his eyes and as he looked at the bleeding form of his Master, he cried *"Fur mich"* (for me). How much did it cost?

"Redeemed"

While on a summer vacation, Dr. A. J. Gordon, that princely preacher of Boston, met a rough country boy who was carrying a heavy iron cage filled with captured birds. "Where and how did you get those poor frightened creatures?" asked Dr. Gordon.

"Oh," said the boy, "here and there in the woods and fields. I caught some; I trapped some; I snared some."

"What are you going to do with them?" inquired Dr. Gordon.

"Oh," said the boy, "I'll play with them for a while, then feed them to the cat."

"Will you sell them to me?" asked the preacher.

"Oh, you don't want them," replied the boy. "They are just common ordinary birds. They aren't worth anything."

"Never mind," said Dr. Gordon. "I know the names of every one of them, and I know their songs. Will you sell them to me?"

"I will," said the boy, "if you will give me my price."

"Name your price," said the Doctor.

"Ten dollars," answered the boy.

Dr. Gordon paid the price and the boy skulked away. The first thing Dr. Gordon did was open that iron door. It had a heavy spring and he had to use his heavy gold-headed cane to get the door open. He jammed the cane into the door so it would not close. One by one the poor frightened creatures at the back and the sides of the cage found the open door and they came out and flew up into God's free heaven. And as each came out, it sang the same song. I know the song: "Redeemed! Redeemed! Redeemed!"

Thank God, Jesus paid the price of our sin. It took nothing less than His Cross to open the door. He put the heavy Cross in the door so that all the devils in hell can never close it. And one by one we poor frightened creatures find the open door, and as we pass through into God's free heaven, we all sing the same song: "Redeemed! Redeemed! Redeemed by the blood of the Lamb!"

Section VI
Divine Ordinances

These are the feasts of the Lord, even holy convocations, which ye shall proclaim in their seasons. In the fourteenth day of the first month at even is the Lord's passover. And on the fifteenth day of the same month is the feast of un-leavened bread unto the Lord: seven days ye must eat un-leavened bread . . . And the Lord spake unto Moses, saying, Speak unto the children of Israel, and say unto them, When ye be come into the land which I give unto you, and shall reap the harvest thereof, then ye shall bring a sheaf of the firstfruits of your harvest unto the priest: and he shall wave the sheaf before the Lord, to be accepted for you: on the morrow after the sabbath the priest shall wave it. And ye shall offer that day when ye wave the sheaf an he lamb without blemish of the first year for a burnt offering unto the Lord . . . And ye shall count unto you from the morrow after the sabbath, from the day that ye brought the sheaf of the wave offering; seven sabbaths shall be complete: even unto the morrow after the seventh sabbath shall ye number fifty days; and ye shall offer a new meat offering unto the Lord. Ye shall bring out of your habitations two wave loaves of two tenth deals: they shall be of fine flour; they shall be baken with leaven; they are the firstfruits unto the Lord. And ye shall offer with the bread seven lambs without blemish of the first year, and one young bullock, and two rams: they shall be for a burnt offering unto the Lord, with their meat offering, and their drink offerings, even an offering made by fire, of sweet savour unto the Lord.

—LEVITICUS 23:4-6, 9-12, 15-18

Section VI: Divine Ordinances

THE FEASTS OF THE LORD

It is often scoffingly said, when we exalt the Holy Bible as the revelation of God, that "God has limited Himself to a book." That scoffing does not bother me in the least, and I would be perfectly willing to admit that God limited Himself to a book because *the Book* is *unlimited*.

But in telling the Gospel story God did not limit Himself to the Bible. He told the Gospel story in divine institutions and ordinances.

Every institution bears the marks of divinity. Every institution of God does two things: (1) it teaches; (2) it proves. It has a didactic property and an apologetic property; that is, it teaches something, and at the same time it proves something.

Both the didactic property and the apologetic property of the institution of the Wilderness Tabernacle have been indicated in the preceding chapters. It is as clear as daylight that the Wilderness Tabernacle is exactly what the ninth chapter of Hebrews says it is: a figure, a pattern, a type, a divinely purposed illustration, or symbol, of Jesus Christ. That is why the furniture was placed in the form of a cross, and why the Golden Candlestick looked forward to Jesus Christ, the Light of the World, and why the Table of Shewbread looked forward to Jesus Christ, the Bread of Life.

It is possible to go into great detail in connection with everything in the Wilderness Tabernacle. We are definitely assured that everything in the Tabernacle was typical; therefore the details must of necessity be received as such.

We could go into detail, for example, in discussing the

bread on the Table of Shewbread as being the type of Christ.
It was unleavened bread because leaven is evil and there was
no evil in the Bread of Life.

How is bread obtained? "Except a corn of wheat fall
into the ground and die, it abideth alone: but if it die, it
bringeth forth much fruit." But what else has to happen
before bread can sustain life? In days gone by the wheat
had to be ground between an upper and a lower millstone.
So the Lord Jesus Christ, before He could become bread
for us, had to be ground between the upper and the lower
millstone. The devils of earth and hell resembled the lower
millstone, and the wrath of God, like the upper millstone,
descended upon His precious head. Furthermore, the wheat
had to be roasted in the oven. So the Lord endured the heat
of the wrath of men and devils, and even of God.

Christ is indeed in every part of the Old Testament Tabernacle. The Tabernacle was placed at the western end of a
great court. This court consisted of white linen curtains, eight
feet high, and there was only one way to approach the Tabernacle: through the one door, or gate, which was at the eastern
end. "There is none other name . . . given among men
whereby we must be saved." "I am the door: by me if any
man enter in, he shall be saved."

Not only does the Wilderness Tabernacle teach the only
approach to God, and that Jesus is the greater and more
perfect tabernacle: it *proves* it. You need only establish,
first, that the Tabernacle existed before Christ—and that
is easy to prove—and, second, look to the pages of history
and prove that Christ existed. Whoever wrote the many
chapters in Exodus and Leviticus concerning the Tabernacle
knew all about Jesus Christ's atonement for sin and the blood
of the Lamb fifteen hundred years before John the Baptist
pointed to the Lord Jesus and cried, "Behold the Lamb of
God, which taketh away the sin of the world."

All God's Old Testament institutions and sacraments
have this didactic and apologetic value: God's New

Testament institutions also have these two values. For instance, the communion service teaches, and at the same time proves, the central fact of the universe, i.e., that the body of the Lord Jesus was broken for us and His blood shed for many for the remission of sins. It teaches this truth and, at the very moment that it teaches it, proves it.

Here is how the communion service proves the death of Christ for us. The communion service as we know it is universal. It is practiced all over the world and has existed for two thousand years. When you have the communion service in your church, other churches in your town, your city, your state, your country, and in the entire world, have it also. Your fathers, grandfathers and great-grandfathers celebrated the communion. It is a universal effect.

Where there is an effect there must be a cause. What is the adequate cause of this effect? You see, do you not? It was the death of the Lord Jesus Christ on the Cross. So by reasoning from the effect to the cause you can prove that the Atonement really happened in history.

Not only does the communion service as we know it prove this great fact of the Atonement: it also performes the second function common to every one of God's institutions: it teaches. God knew that wolves clothed in sheepskins would find their way into the pulpits and corrupt the flock, but He placed the central fact of the Gospel in an institution in such a way as to force these racketeers to tell the Gospel story in objective form whether they wanted to or not, and any child can see that the broken bread symbolizes the broken body of Christ and the poured-out wine represents the blood of our Saviour.

Now, entering the realm of Christian apologetics, I am going to point you to the seven institutions, or sacraments, or feasts, that God Almighty ordained as they are recorded in Leviticus 23. This chapter contains seven monuments which are a complete story of the death, the burial and the resurrection of Jesus Christ and the founding of the Christian

Church on the Day of Pentecost! All this is found in the
ancient book of Leviticus written 1490 B.C.!

Leviticus 23 contains a list of the seven Feasts of Jehovah.
They are almost identical to the seven holidays on the Jewish
calendar today. The blind Jew does not know that every
time he keeps one of these feasts he is telling the story of
Jesus Christ's death, burial and resurrection.

We, being human, established a holy day, or holiday, to
celebrate something that has already occurred in our history.
The Fourth of July, for example, is set aside as a holiday,
and it declares that we gained independence on that day. In
France, July 14 is known as Bastille Day, and that holiday
marks the beginning of the French Revolution. November
11, our Armistic Day, commemorates the ending of the
First World War. But because we are human, our holidays
celebrate only something that *has happened.*

"Christ, Our Passover"

But God, being God, makes His holidays symbolize something that did happen and something that is *going to happen,*
and He begins the calendar of the Jewish year with the
Passover, as we read in Leviticus 23:5. The Jews were to take
a spotless lamb, which met all the specifications mentioned
in this book, shed its blood, put the blood on the top and the
sides of the doorposts, and then put the basin of blood on the
threshold. (Thus the sign of the Cross was made with the
blood of a Passover lamb, and Christ is called specifically
in the epistles "our passover . . . sacrificed for us." The
Hebrew word for "basin" and for "threshold" is the same.)

God said on that first terrible night of the Passover,
"When I see the blood, I will pass over you," and that held
good then, and it holds good now, and it will hold good
forever.

The Passover was the first of a series of seven holidays on
the calendar of the Jew and it looked forward to Christ. The
second holy day mentioned in Leviticus 23 is indicated in the

sixth verse; it was "the feast of unleavened bread." This feast, of course, looked forward to Christ, the Bread of Life, who had no leaven or evil in Him.

"CHRIST . . . THE FIRSTFRUITS OF THEM THAT SLEPT"

The third holy day, or holiday, was the Feast of the Firstfruits. This feast is described in Leviticus 23:9-12. A male lamb, with all the usual qualifications, was killed. The priest lifted it as an offering to the Lord, and, of course, this foreshadowed the death of the Lamb of God for us. But something else happened on that day. The priest waved a sheaf of wheat before the Lord. A sheaf of wheat has always been a symbol of resurrection. The death and the resurrection of Christ were dramatized in that ritual. Sometimes the priest was instructed to make a "heave offering," that is, he lifted the sacrifice up and down in a virtical position, and then he was instructed to make a "wave offering," that is, he moved the offering as far as he could to his left and then to his right. Again, the heave and the wave offerings formed the sign of the Cross.

Here is an amazing fact. On what day of the week was the Feast of the Firstfruits to be held? Leviticus 23:11 gives the answer. The Feast of the Firstfruits was to be celebrated on "the morrow after the sabbath"! That is Sunday. The feast, therefore, looked forward to Easter.

For a Jew to receive instructions from God to observe a holy day on "the morrow after the sabbath" would be the same as for you and me to think of Monday or Tuesday as a holy day. There would seem to be "no sense to it." But now, looking back, we see plainly that God was thinking of Sunday, the Lord's Day, and the Resurrection Day. God did not select Sunday arbitrarily. A Jew had to observe the Feast of the Firstfruits on Sunday even though his own inclination would be to celebrate it on the Sabbath Day, Saturday. How can the Jew be so blind as not to see the blessed Lord Jesus

Christ in every institution and in every sacrifice that God Almighty directed!

Certainly it is true "that blindness in part is happened to Israel, until the fulness of the Gentiles be come in." Alert in all other fields, the Jew is blind to spiritual truths. He can see the Golden Candlestick and never see the Light of the World. He can see the Golden Table of Shewbread and never see Christ, the Bread of Life. He can look at the bleeding lamb and the precious blood and never see the Lamb slain from the foundation of the world. He can read all the detailed instructions regarding the Passover lamb and never see Christ our Pasover, sacrificed for us. He can observe the instructions to keep the Feast of the Firstfruits on Sunday and never see Christ "the firstfruits" who rose on Sunday.

At the Passover, even to this day, the Jewish father takes three pieces of unleavened bread. Suppose I ask a Jew, "Why unleavened bread?" He sayes, "I do not know," so I declare, "I will tell you. Because the bread looks forward to the Bread with no evil in it—the Lord Jesus Christ."

"Why do you take three pieces?" I ask. "I don't know," replies the Jew. "I will tell you. To represent the Father, the Son and the Holy Ghost," I explain. Now the Jew takes the second wafer and breaks it. "Why do you break the second wafer?" I ask. "I don't know," says the Jew. "All right, I will tell you. Because it was the Second Person of the Godhead whose body was broken for you." The Jew then hides the broken wafer in a napkin and puts it on the table, and sometime during the meal the youngest child must "steal" that broken wafer out of the napkin. The Passover meal ends with the father's playfully opening the napkin and declaring that the wafer is gone.

The Jew has no idea why he does these things. If it were not for his spiritual blindness he could see that the Feast of the Firstfruits is a dramatization of the death, the burial, the resurrection and the empty tomb of the Lord Jesus Christ.

Again—do not forget that the Feast of the Firstfruits was held on "the morrow after the sabbath." Are you ready to admit that God was thinking of the Resurrection Day of His beloved Son?

Let us consider now the Feast of Pentecost. In Leviticus 23:15-17 God says, "And ye shall count unto you from the morrow after the sabbath, from the day that ye brought the sheaf of the wave offering; seven sabbaths shall be complete: even unto the morrow after the seventh sabbath shall ye number fifty days; and ye shall offer a new meat offering unto the Lord. Ye shall bring out of your habitations two wave loaves of two tenth deals: they shall be of fine flour; they shall be baken *with leaven;* they are the firstfruits unto the Lord."

Why again the phrase "the morrow after the . . . sabbath," and "fifty days"? This period of time terminated on another Sunday. Fifty days after Easter Sunday the Church of Jesus Christ was born!

Why is leaven mentioned? Throughout the Bible, leaven is a symbol of evil. An Israelite hated leaven, and was told to hate it. At the Passover season the wife of an Israelite ransacked her house from top to bottom, cellar to attic, to make sure there was no leaven in her home. The housewife reported to her husband that there was no leaven in the house, but, nevertheless, the head of the house lit a candle (and the practice has continued to this day), inspected every room, and came to the front door of his house and said aloud, "There is no leaven in my house. And if there is one bit of leaven in my dwelling, it is here against my will."

That is how an Israelite regarded leaven, everywhere, always, and continually. "Beware of the leaven of the . . . Sadducees," said the Lord Jesus. Why did God say, in Leviticus, to celebrate a certain day fifty days after the Feast of the Firstfruits and "the morrow after the . . . sabbath"? And why celebrate it with loaves of bread "baked with leaven"? God was looking ahead to what was going to happen on Easter when the blessed Lord Jesus was going to rise from the dead, and He was also thinking of His Church, which was going to be born fifty days after Easter—the Church which would have evil in it from the beginning to the very end!

The remaining feasts were: the Feast of Trumpets (Leviticus 23:24) and the great Day of Atonement (Leviticus 23:27), when the high priest entered the Holy of Holies with the blood of atonement which looked forward to our High Priest who entered heaven for us with His own blood. The seventh and last was the Feast of Tabernacles (Leviticus 23:33), looking forward, of course, to the arrival of the Church at our final dwelling place in heaven with God.

Each of the feasts, like all God's institutions, teach and prove.

THE TABERNACLE PROVES THE BIBLE

This book on the Wilderness Tabernacle is not intended to be a textbook on Christian apologetics, but by this time you must have noticed how wonderfully and conclusively the Wilderness Tabernacle *proves* the Bible. Certainly it is very plain that "in the Old Testament the New Testament lies enfolded, and in the New Testament the Old Testament lies unfolded." This being true, the case for the authenticity and the genuineness of the Scriptures is closed, and prewar German "higher" criticism falls to the ground.

Through the Neuremberg trials, the gigantic mobilization of German scholarship under Goebbels, and by the confession of Bretchsnider and others even before World War I, we know that since Bismark, German life, and especially the German educational system, has been under the domination of the German military party.

Since 1870 the military party has controlled the colleges and the universities of Germany. Hitler and Goebbels went so far as to control even the grammer schools and the kindergartens.

From Bismarck to Hitler the military party has known that there is only one way for a party to control a nation. It must control not only the bodies but the minds and the very *souls* of men. In order to do this the military party has had to break all authority but that emanating from the German general staff.

Such a program demands the elimination of all other authorities, even the authority of Deity; and so "God must be banished from the skies and capitalism from the earth." In order to blast God from the minds of the people it is necessary to blast His Book. And there lies the alpha and the omega of German higher criticism.

The higher critics' scheme rested on the granting or withholding of the higher academic degrees. If the thesis of a scholar were accepted, the scholar received his degree. If the thesis were not accepted, the degree was withheld. Long before World War I, and at the peak of German higher criticism, it became evident that a thesis, in theology, for instance, had to be a "contribution." It had to be something which had not been "done before," so, of course, any thesis that supported the Old Testament was not a "contribution"; but a thesis that denied the Old Testament was a "contribution" and therefore acceptable, and the degree was granted.

This explains the flood of books on German higher criticism. Most students will agree that the greatest book of the higher critics was Bretchsnider's *Probabilia*. The *Probabilia* is a scholarly discussion attacking the authenticity and the genuineness of the Fourth Gospel. The German critic's work is only a little volume, but it made me wade through what seemed to be all the books ever written about the Gospel of John. I respected Bretchsnider's scholarship. I thought that the *Probabilia* was a serious piece of scholarly investigation. I did not know, however, that Bretchsnider was only "kidding" and that in his later volumes on John he admits that he wrote the *Probabilia* for "academic reasons" and "to provoke thought," and that never has he doubted for a single moment the authenticity and the genuineness of the blessed Gospel of John.

Goebbels developed control over the thought-life of Germany. This German leader must go down in history as the world's greatest liar. We know that he actually mobilized and organized no less than ten thousand university professors into a veritable lie factory. They "re-edited" the encyclopedias, the histories, the geographies and even the dictionary and the Bible. The only thing the Nazis left untouched was the multiplication table. The dreadful book-burnings all over Germany during the rise of the Nazi Party were systematic and terrible. This shows why we have and shall have a very serious problem with regard to German youth. The same is true of Russia, where all the books, the encyclopedias and the histories in the libraries are "supervised," and no book is allowed without the official stamp of the Kremlin.

Sir Willian Ramsay, once perhaps himself the greatest of German higher critics, sums up the case for higher criticism. "In the light of recent archæological discoveries a skeptical attitude toward the Old Testament is now a sign of ignorance or of near--knowledge."

If only we had concentrated on the Bible itself, and not on books *about* the Bible, we would never have gotten into the deplorable state in which the world finds itself today.

Let us look directly into the blessed Book itself and see how it proves itself.

As we have seen, every color, object, position, dimension, sacrifice and ceremony in the Wilderness Tabernacle pointed forward to Christ. Christ is the Tabernacle, the Lamb, the High Priest, the Door, the Bread of Life, the Light of the World. Even the things God left *out* of the Tabernacle pointed forward to Christ. We have seen the beautiful reason why a floor was omitted. But why was there no chair in the Tabernacle? One might expect at least one beautiful chair to be among the furniture of any building. But the chair is conspicuous for its absence in the ancient Tabernacle. Why? Because under the old covenant the work of a priest was never done. This fact spoke of the great High Priest who cried on the Cross, "It is finished."

Why was there no green, brown, or gray among the colors in the Tabernacle? Because green and brown and gray are earth colors, not heavenly colors, and the Wilderness Tabernacle looked forward to and symbolized the Heavenly Tabernacle, Jesus Christ. Therefore the earth colors did not appear, but the heavenly colors—gold, blue, purple, scarlet and white fine-twined linen—were present.

A detailed study of the Wilderness Tabernacle and its services will reveal some seventy definite features which harmonize with the Lord Jesus Christ and His wondrous salvation.

THE LAW OF MATHEMATICAL PROBABILITY

These seventy features of the Tabernacle bring us into a very solid realm—mathematics. Mathematics is considered the only perfect science. This subject includes the study of permutations and the "law of mathematical probability."

The laws of mathematical probability are as reliable as the laws of gravity and motion. Insurance companies and large financial institutions are built upon the laws of mathematical probability, and if these laws should fail, all the great insurance companies and financial institutions of the world would collapse immediately.

I am surprised that this law is not more often applied to the claims of Christianity. By applying it one can produce a mighty argument for the truth of the Word of God.

So many features of the Wilderness Tabernacle coincide so perfectly with characteristics of the Lord Jesus Christ that the law of mathematical probability would forbid that they be chance happenings. Furthermore, there are hundreds of direct prophecies in the Major and Minor Prophets telling how, where, when and of what ancestry and from what family the Lord Jesus would come, and how He would die and rise again.

The addition of all these points about the Wilderness Tabernacle to all the Messianic prophecies of the Major and Minor Prophets produces a large figure. And when we place beside all these Old Testament predictions the actual history of Christ, we find a perfect and amazing harmony. This presents a mathematical and historical argument that is overwhelming.

Could Jesus Christ, even if He had wanted to, have arranged, as a mere human being, to have himself born in Bethlehem where the Prophet Micah declared the Christ would be born? Could He have arranged to appear as the Messiah at the exact time when the Prophet Daniel declared the Messiah would appear? Could He have arranged to have Himself born into the nation, the tribe and the family that the prophets predicted?

Ask yourself this question, and face the inevitable answer. Could Jesus Christ possibly have fashioned His life and work and nature so as to fit perfectly into the more than seventy features of the Wilderness Tabernacle and its services? Could He make John the Baptist point Him out as the Lamb of God? No human being could control John the Baptist. Even King Herod tried that and failed.

See on what solid ground our faith rests! God does not ask us to believe until He gives us many infallible proofs. These seventy features of the Tabernacle are like the seventy pieces of a jigsaw puzzle. After you have patiently put them together they form a perfect picture of Christ. You must conclude that "someone intended it that way."

THE TESTIMONY OF HISTORY

The claims of Christianity also rest upon history. History is also a science. Science is the classification of exact knowledge. Tradition is a record of more or less imperfect knowledge, but history is a record of what actually happened and can be proved to have happened. It is on such a basis that the claims of Christianity rest.

The Lord Jesus Christ was a *public* man. He lived, loved, labored and died in a blaze of publicity. Paul says significantly to King Agrippa, "This thing was not done in a corner." By proving that the Old Testament existed before Christ, which is, of course, exceedingly easy, and then that the main public events in the life of Christ actually occurred (which is equally easy), one can establish the claims of Christianity.

STARTLING MATHEMATICS

Let us consider further the law of mathematical probability. What chance would there be for all the features (the lamb, the Tabernacle and the hundreds of direct prophecies about Christ)—what chance would there be for all these to coincide *by accident* with the characteristics of the Lord Jesus Christ?

Let me show you something about the laws of chance. Suppose you put ten books in a row on a shelf in a certain order, and then the books were shuffled. What would be the chance of putting them back again in the same order? You would have one chance in 3,628,800. There are that many transpositions possible with ten. You can begin to grasp this fact a bit when you see how many different words you can spell and how many letter combinations you can obtain by rearranging ten letters of the alphabet. You can understand it also when you consider the many melodies you can form from seven whole notes in music. To find the number of transpositions possible with ten books, figure thus: $1 \times 2 \times 3 \times 4 \times 5 \times 6 \times 7 \times 8 \times 9 \times 10$ equals 3,628,800 In the case of the seven notes, $1 \times 2 \times 3 \times 4 \times 5 \times 6 \times 7$ equals 5,250.

Let me use another illustration. This will show you from a mathematical standpoint why certain things *cannot* happen by chance. Suppose your child is playing on the floor with five little *ABC* blocks. Each of these blocks has of course, six letters, making a total of thirty letters. Suppose that you arrange these blocks on the floor so that *J* is on one, *E* on another, *S* on another, *U* on another and *S* on the fifth. In other words, the five blocks are in such an order as to spell the Name "Jesus." Then you shuffle the blocks, turn up other letters at random, and change the order completely. A stranger who does not know the original order or arrangement of the blocks is invited to arrange these blocks by chance. What possibility would he have, on the basis of mere chance, to arrange these blocks so as to spell the word "Jesus"? He would have exactly one chance in 620,448,401, 735,259,493,369,000! That is, he would have exactly one chance in six sextillion because there are that many transpositions possible with thirty letters!

And that is just about how much "chance" there would be for all the wondrous features of the Wilderness Tabernacle to spell the wondrous Name of Jesus by accident. The little spotless male lamb spelled "Jesus"; the Tabernacle spelled "Jesus"; the high priest spelled "Jesus"; all the sacrifices spelled "Jesus." If you wanted to carry this out mathematically, it would bring you into infinity, and that is exactly where it does bring you—right up to the infinite God, who showed Moses the wondrous Tabernacle from the Holy Mount and ordered him to make on the earth a pattern of what he saw in the infinities.

I am weary of hearing people say that things "happen by chance," instead of giving God Almighty the honor that is His due. First Corinthians 10:11 declares, "All these things happened unto [the Israelites] for ensamples [types]: and they are for our admonition, upon whom the ends of the world are come."

Let's return to the poor fellow arranging blocks on the floor Suppose he continued to arrange the blocks and made one transposition per second. It would take one man 1,967, 428,975,879,120 years to make all the possible transpositions with the blocks, since there are more than six sextillion transpositions possible with thirty letters!

A study of permutations, probability and compound probability will make it plain why we say that certain things cannot "happen by chance." I wonder what an American Beauty rose would look like if it were produced by "chance." What would *you* look like, with your hundreds of muscles, and bones, and organs, if "chance" produced you? Your eyes would perhaps be on the top of your head, so that when you put your hat on you could not see. Or your nose might be on the top of your head, so that every time you sneezed you would blow your hat off.

I wonder who planned the Wilderness Tabernacle. I wonder who made those eleven specifications regarding the Passover lamb. I wonder who painted the flowers and the birds and the sunset, and ordered the stars and the planets. I wonder who ordained that on the shell of every chicken egg there should be a little spot softer than the rest, and located precisely where the little chick's beak is going to be. Did someone know that the little fellow would need help as he crashed his way into this wonderful world? Near the new little chick's new little beak is a pocket of air—which is nowhere else in the egg. Did this "happen by chance"?

I wonder why "chance" makes a very arbitrary exception in the contraction and expansion of water. Everything under the sun—liquids, solids, or gases—contracts on cooling and expands on heating, and continues to contract with more cooling or to expand with more heating. Even water expands exactly upon heating and contracts exactly upon cooling, but when it gets down to a certain point, water refuses to follow this procedure. It behaves in orthodox fashion to a certain point, and then suddenly it refuses to contract. Nothing else in all the universe—liquids, solids, or gasses—behaves like that, but at 32 degrees water simply will not contract. In fact, the more you cool it, the more it expands.

What happens? Can it be that someone is thinking about

the fish and the vegetation that would die if water continued to contract? That is exactly what would happen. If water would contract, get heavier, and sink, the fish would die. Is someone arbitrarily making an exception in the case of water? Yes, Someone is thinking of the fish and the vegetation. You will remember that He said He takes note of the sparrow's fall.

As we have indicated, the potency of numbers in simple permutations is staggering. Enormous totals are reached by geometric progression and ordinary transposition.

We all remember the blacksmith who shod the king's horse according to the agreement that the smith was to receive one cent for the first nail, two cents for the second, four cents for the third, eight cents for the fourth, and so on. Eventually the king was penniless and the blacksmith became a millionaire! There is another story, mathematically correct, about the boy who hired himself out on the basis of one cent for the first day, two cents for the second, four cents for the third, and then doubling for each day for a month. For the last day of the month the boy's wages were $5,368,709.12 and he received for the entire month $10,737,418.23.

Sir Isaac Newton

While we are considering mathematics and the Bible, let me cite one more example. For this I have the support of the greatest mathematician who ever lived, Sir Isaac Newton. The French Academy five times voted Sir Isaac "the greatest brain the human race has ever produced."

Many of the ministers I have met throughout America and Canada are surprised to find that Sir Isaac Newton was a devout worshiper of Christ and great earnest student of the Bible. Newton spent more time with his Bible than with his study of physics.

Newton had many debates on religion with the famous French philosopher Voltaire, who ridiculed Newton by sneering, "See how the brain of a real scientist softens when he leaves his own field and goes into the field of religion." One time, attempting to ridicule Sir Isaac Newton's faith in Daniel 12:4, "Many shall run to and fro, and knowledge shall be increased," Voltaire said, "Mr. Newton declares that the time will come when mankind will travel over the earth at the rate of sixy miles per hour. Anybody knows that no man could even breathe if he traveled at that rate of speed." We wonder what the great Voltaire would have said if he had known that only a century after his time any high-school boy would be disgusted with a jalopy that would not travel at least sixty miles per hour! What would Voltaire have said had he known about the speed of today's airplanes?

To Sir Isaac Newton and to Sir Robert Anderson I am indebted for the following mathematical prediction of the exact time of the manifestation of Jesus Christ the Messiah.

DANIEL PREDICTS THE VERY YEAR FOR THE MANIFESTATION
OF THE MESSIAH

A careful study of the facts here presented, a consideration of the Old Testament passages indicated, and a check with the dates of secular history will prove that the date set for the manifestation of the Messiah was predicted to the very month, April, 32 A.D.

Daniel says that in chapter 9:25 "Know therefore and understand that from the going forth of the commandment to restore and to rebuild Jerusalem unto the Messiah the Prince shall be seven weeks of years, and three-score and two weeks of years." I have given the translation "weeks of years" because it is so given in Moffatt's translation and all lexicons.

The Hebrew word here is *heptads*. It means "sevens," and indicates a week of seven days or years, according to the context in which it is found. In Daniel 9 it indicates a week of years. In Genesis 29 it has a similar function. Jacob worked seven years to earn Rachel, so agreed to work another "week," and Rachel's mercenary father said, "Finish thy week, and take Rachel also." The passage concludes: "So Jacob served him yet seven other years" for Rachel.

Daniel 9 says that the Messiah would appear sixty-nine year-weeks, or 483 years, after "the going forth of the commandment to restore and to build Jerusalem." This commandment was given by King Artaxerxes in the twentieth year of his reign and in the month of Nisan, which is part of our March and April. Nehemiah describes the giving of this commandment, and gives its date in his second chapter, which begins thus: "And it came to pass in the month Nisan, in the twentieth year of Artaxerxes the king, that wine was before him: and I took up the wine, and gave it unto the king. Now I had not been beforetime sad in his presence. Wherefore the king said unto me, Why is thy countenance sad?"

Nehemiah was a captive Jew employed as cupbearer to King Artaxerxes. Nisan was Passover season, and the captive Jew was thinking wistfully of his own beloved Jerusalem, then in ruins. Artaxerxes wanted to grant his servant a favor, and issued a formal decree to allow Nehemiah to go and build the Holy City. To make it still more official, Nehemiah 2:6 says that the queen was sitting by the king. At that time Artaxerxes was the most powerful monarch in the world.

The Bible is a wonderful Book. When it goes into detail regarding dates and other facts, there is always a reason— this time a tremendous reason, because Daniel the prophet had said in his ninth chapter that in exactly 483 years, after the going forth of the commandment to restore and to build Jerusalem," the Messiah would appear.

We have the exact date for the going forth of that commandment, a date established by both secular and sacred history. It was the twentieth year of Artaxerxes, in the month of Nisan. The *New International Encyclopedia* states that Artaxerxes began to reign in 465 B.C. The twentieth year of his reign was, therefore, 445 B.C.

The exact date of the birth of Jesus Christ, and the exact

date for His formal entrance into Jerusalem on Palm Sunday, are established from the second and third chapters of Luke. In Luke 2:1-2 we observe the exactness of dates again, and the names of men who were universally known, such as Caesar Augustus, who ordered a universal tax when Cyrenius was governor of Syria. And in Luke 3:1-2 we have another fixed date—the fifteenth year of the reign of Tiberius Caesar, in which year Pontius Pilate was governor of Judea, and Herod, tetrarch of Galilee, and Herod's brother Philip, tetrarch of Iturea, which coincided with the time when Lysanias was tetrarch of Abilene, and which also coincided with the time when Annas and Caiaphas were high priests and John the Baptist was preaching in the wilderness.

The Bible is marvelously accurate. Most of the so-called negative "higher critics" of prewar days admit that now. If the Bible ever made any contradictions, they would not be trivial. They would be very serious contradictions, because dates, names and places are repeated and recorded in the most daring and detailed specific fashion. Truth alone writes like that. And in this particular case the Holy Spirit, who is Truth, has given us great help. We know beyond the peradventure of a doubt the date for the going forth of the commandment to restore and to build Jerusalem. It was Nisan, 445 B.C. There was another decree issued by Cyrus to build the Temple, but the decree of Artaxerxes is the only one on record to build the city: and it is concerning the building of the city that Daniel 9 speaks.

We know the exact date of the first Palm Sunday, when Jesus Christ offered Himself formally as the Messiah. It was the fourth Passover of His ministry, April 6, 32 A.D., according to the Julian calendar.

Calculations from the Nehemiah date, Nisan, 445 B.C., to Nisan, 32 A.D., show exactly 483 Jewish years. Remember that the Jewish was 360 days, twelve thirty-day months.

The rest of the passage in Daniel 9 gives a description of what would happen to the Messiah when He did come: He would be killed. Then the passage states that after the Crucifixion the city would be destroyed by the people of the prince of whom other parts of Daniel speak as coming upon the stage of the world in the time that is known as Daniel's seventieth week. The passage closes by mentioning what our Lord said would characterize future history, namely, "wars and desolations."

The whole of this remarkable prophecy is contained in two verses, and reads as follows: "Know therefore and understand, that from the going forth of the commandment to restore and to build Jerusalem unto the Messiah the Prince shall be seven year-weeks, and threescore and two year-weeks: the street shall be built again, and the wall, even in troublous times. And after threescore and two year-weeks shall the Messiah be cut off." (Christ was crucified five days after His formal offer of Himself as the Messiah. Note that the prophecy does not say the Crucifixion would take place *within* that sixty-nine-year-week period of 483 years, but *after*.) "And will have nothing: and the people of the prince that shall come shall destroy the city and the sanctuary." (Jerusalem was destroyed by the Romans forty years later.) "And unto the end, wars and desolations are determined." (Wars and desolations have been the order of the day ever since, and still are [Daniel 9:25-26].)

Mathematicians who are interested will find that Daniel's prophecy is not only "close" but exact, to the month, and perhaps to the day. Note that from 1 B.C. to 1 A.D. is one year, and not two, and remember, again, that the Jewish year was the conventional year of 360 days. If we dare to assume one thing, namely, that the decree recorded by Nehemiah went forth on the first day of the Passover week, which is very likely, that would set the date for the going forth of the commandment—March 14, 445 B.C.. The calculations then are correct to the very day. What we know about the date for the issuing of the commandment to build Jerusalem is that it was Nisan, 445 B.C. The only thing we are assuming is that Nehemiah was sad in the presence of the king because it was the Passover week of the month of Nisan, and the first day, for he was an exile far from his beloved Jerusalem.

With due consideration of the changes that have taken place in the calendar during the last twenty-five hundred years, and with consideration also of the care with which the Jews have always celebrated the Passover and the Sabbath, no matter where they were, we find that the first day of Passover week, 445 B.C., was March 14. The finished quotation will then be as follows: from 445 B.C. to 32 A.D. is 476 years. When this is turned into days, by multiplying 476 by 365, it is 173,740 days. To these 173,740 days must be added 116 days for leap years, because there were that many leap years in that period of time. Twenty-four days must be added to cover the time elapsing between March 14 to April 6. We then have a total of 173,880 days. And if the 173,880 days are divided by 360, the answer is exactly 483 years, which is the same as sixty-nine Jewish year-weeks!

I challenge any man to combat these historical and mathematical statements in Daniel 9, Nehemiah 2 and Luke 1 and 3. No fact is "stretched" or "forced." I am simply putting before you the facts as taken from the Bible, lexicons, Hebrew grammers and almanacs. I have not found one Hebrew scholar, Modernistic or otherwise, who gives any translation of Daniel's word for "week" other than that it means, in the context in which it is found, a period of seven years. You will profit from a careful consideration of these facts, for in this amazing prophecy we have the date for the formal appearance of the Messiah exactly predicted to the year and month, and very likely to the day.

Section VII

The Holy Communion

For I have received of the Lord that which also I delivered unto you, That the Lord Jesus the same night in which he was betrayed took bread: and when he had given thanks, he brake it, and said, Take, eat: this is my body, which is broken for you: this do in remembrance of me. After the same manner also he took the cup, when he had supped, saying, This cup is the new testament in my blood: this do ye, as oft as ye drink it, in remembrance of me. For as often as ye eat this bread, and drink this cup, ye do shew the Lord's death till he come. Wherefore whosoever shall eat this bread, and drink this cup of the Lord, unworthily, shall be guilty of the body and blood of the Lord. But let a man examine himself, and so let him eat of that bread, and drink of that cup. For he that eateth and drinketh unworthily, eateth and drinketh damnation to himself, not discerning the Lord's body. For this cause many are weak and sickly among you, and many sleep. For if we would judge ourselves, we should not be judged. But when we are judged, we are chastened of the Lord, that we should not be condemned with the world.

—I CORINTHIANS 11:23-32

Section VII: The Holy Communion

I have gone into great detail regarding the institutions of God because I want to show you that they have the earmarks of divinity. They are holy; they are Godlike; they are sacred. The old covenant has disappeared now and has been fulfilled in the new covenant, but there are two great sacraments for the Church Age: communion and baptism.

The communion service is connected with the Wilderness Tabernacle institution. In fact, the Wilderness Tabernacle was the Old Testament communion service. The communion service is the New Testament, or the new covenant, service. Its importance cannot be axaggerated.

I propose to show, on Biblical grounds, why many godly people have suffered, and will continue to suffer, sickness, physical weakness and even death. I propose to show, also on Biblical grounds, how some of this sickness, physical weakness and premature death can be avoided.

I call your attention to I Corinthians 11:23-32 which has been read altogether too glibly. There is a faithful warning here about eating and drinking the body and the blood of the Lord unworthily. In fact, we are told that when we approach a communion service in an improper manner, and without self-judgment, we are eating and drinking damnation! "For he that eateth and drinketh unworthily, eateth and drinketh damnation to himself, not discerning the Lord's body. For this cause many are weak and sickly among you, and many sleep," say verses 29 and 30 of I Corinthians 11. "For if we should judge ourselves, we should not be judged. But when we are judged, we are chastened of the Lord, that we should not be condemned with the world." So declare verses 31 and 32 of the same chapter.

I want it understood that I shall not attempt to explain all the reasons for suffering and sickness among God's people. There are mysteries about this which are not revealed, and we shall have to wait until eternity before we can have a full and complete explanation as to why godly people suffer.

But I do insist that I Corinthians 11:23 declares why "many are weak and sickly among you, and many sleep," and I further insist that the thiry-first and thirty-second verses declare that some of the sickness, physical weakness and even death can be avoided if we judge ourselves *before* we come to communion, rather than wait for God to judge us. If we wait and make it necessary for Him to judge us, chastisement will follow, "that we should not be condemned with the world." The very fact that we belong to God and are children of God puts us in line for chastisement, unless we judge ourselves. If we were not born-again children of God, but bastards, as Hebrews 12 declares, then He would not chastise us. But declares the same chapter, whom He "loveth he chasteneth."

Be it known to you from now on that even though you are born again you are still dealing with a holy God, and any carelessness or neglect will lead to chastisement, unless you judge yourself.

It is very well to think of God as Father, but God is more than the Father of the faithful. He is the moral Governor of the universe, and He is absolutely holy. There are two sides to God: love for righteousness, and infinite wrath for evil of any kind. It is a fearful thing to fall into the hands of an angry God. Even angels were cast out of heaven by the holy God. Twenty-three thousand of the chosen people were slaughtered by God in one day. "The wicked shall be turned into hell, and all the nations that forget God." The holy Temple at Jerusalem was leveled to the ground by the wrath of God. Not one stone was left upon another. The Chosen

People have been scattered to every nation under the sun for two thousand years, as exiled wanderers.

God is the Creator of this entire universe. You are dealing with Him. The sun is ninty-three million miles away. Light, which travels at the rate of 182,000 miles a second, takes nine full minutes to get here from the sun. But the North Star is so far away that forty-five years are required for its light to reach our earth. Sir William Herschel, of the London Observatory, declares that there are stars which can be measured and weighed, and they are 28,000 times farther from the earth than the North Star. The known universe (to say nothing of that part which is unknown)— the known universe is so vast that light speeding at the rate of 182,000 miles a second requires 15,000,000 years to flash across the known diameter once.

You are dealing with the Creator of these wonders, and that Creator is absolutely holy. He condescended to dwell in the Holy of Holies, behind curtains. He allowed the high priests to approach Him once a year "not without blood." The high priest had two sons, Nadab and Abihu. They did not go into the Holy of Holies but they did go into the Holy Place apart from God, and the holiness of God burned them to cinders, and the children of Israel buried them. You are dealing with the God before whom the four and twenty elders cast their golden crowns upon the glassy sea, and before whom the four living creatures cease not day or night to cry, "Holy, holy, holy." That is the God with whom you communed at your last communion service. Did you thoroughly judge yourself before you touched that sacred bread and before you lifted that sacred cup to your lips? If you did not judge yourself, that bread and that cup were poison for you, and according to I Corinthians 11:29, you ate and drank damnation to yourself.

I am not trying to frighten you, if you are a born-again Christian, by telling you that you are in danger of eternal damnation. If you are truly saved, you are not in danger of eternal damnation. But if you are saved, and not continually judging and confessing your sins, then you are in immediate danger of *temporal* damnation. If you are unsaved, let me warn you never to look at the Cross of Jesus Christ again and say, "How soft God is," or "How easy God is." But fall down on your face and cry, "How shall we escape, if we neglect so great salvation?"

A word of caution is needed here for people who "think" they are saved. Salvation is tremendously serious. If you are saved you have the birthmarks of the new birth on you. They are given in the First Epistle of John: (1) he that is born of God sinneth not; (2) he that is born of God doeth righteousness; (3) he that is born of God loveth the brethren.

You are saying perhaps, that this is a heretical statement because the Word of God says, "Believe on the Lord Jesus Christ, and thou shalt be saved." No one believes that more than I do. But the question I want to ask you is: Do you really believe? Or is it a mere profession? If it is genuine belief, it is followed by good works. If the good works do not follow, then you have merely profession. I can settle this entire matter of faith and works in one sentence: *The test of your salvation is your faith, but the test of your faith is your works.*

Suppose I secure the services of the Philadelphia Symphony Orchestra and declare that anybody can be admitted free to the Carnegie Hall concert on one condition, namely, that he makes some kind of musical contribution on some sort of musical intrument. The concert is for musicians only, and to enter, one must play a few bars of music. One fellow comes to the gate and plays very sweetly a few measures on the violin, and the judges say, "Admit him; he has contributed a bit of music." Another comes and plays still more wonderfully. He, too, is admitted. Another comes who has very little ability, but still he can produce something that passes for music. He, too, is admitted, but a fourth man comes along, picks up a violin, starts scratching on it, and then, pleading that he has produced music, tries to push through the gate. But the judges will not let him pass. "Why not?" he asks. "Doesn't the sign say that if you play a little music the admission is free?" "Yes," the judges say, "and that is the one and only condition for entrance to this concert hall, but you did not produce music." Then the infuriated would-be musician scratches louder than ever on his violin, and demands, "Let me in. This is music." "No," say the judges, "that is not music: that is *noise.*"

There will be many disappointments in eternity. Some people will cry "Lord, Lord," and the Judge of all the universe will say, "I never knew you," and others will cry, "Lord, Lord have we not . . . in thy name done many wonderful works?" and the Judge will reply, "Depart from me, ye that work iniquity."

"Lord, are there few that be saved?" asked the disciples of Jesus one day. And the answer came, "Strait is the gate, and narrow is the way . . . and few there be that find it." "Lord, are there few that be saved?" The answer comes, "Work out your own salvation with fear and trembling. For it is God which worketh in you." "Lord, are there few that be saved?" The answer comes, "Make your calling and election sure. Have an abundant entrance into the kingdom of God."

Of the millions of people on the earth in the antediluvian days, how many were really saved with Noah? Eight. Of the hundreds of thousands who wandered through the Wilderness with Moses, how many got into the Promised Land? Two. Joshua and Caleb. Of all the people in Sodom and Gomorrah, how many were spared? Lot and his family. Of two and one-fourth million acorns, how many acorns became oak trees? The answer of biology is: one. Of a million rose seeds, how many become rose bushes? The answer is: one. If we see how God works in biology, and how God works in history, we may well work out our "own salvation with fear and trembling."

If you are really saved, then you are not in danger of

eternal damnation, but unless you are living continually in the Holy of Holies, and washing and cleansing yourself, and judging yourself at the Brazen Laver in front of the Tabernacle of God, you are in immediate danger of temporal damnation.

I will tell you how you can avoid a great many headaches and heartaches between here and heaven. I live next door to Mrs. Billy Sunday, and when we start on an evangelistic campaign, Mrs. Sunday acts as our alarm clock and wakes us and we have breakfast in our cottage together, and then read Billy Sunday's favorite Psalm, the Thirty-fourth. Five verses in that Psalm read as follows: "What man is he that desireth life, and loveth many days, that he may see good? Keep thy tongue from evil, and thy lips from speaking guile. Depart from evil, and do good; seek peace, and pursue it. The eyes of the Lord are upon the righteous, and his ears are open unto their cry. The face of the Lord is against them that do evil, to cut off the remembrance of them from the earth." First Peter 3 makes almost the same declaration beginning at verse 10, "For he that will live life, and see good days, let him refrain his tongue from evil, and his lips that they speak no guile: let him eschew evil, and do good; let him seek peace, and ensue it. For the eyes of the Lord are over the righteous, and his ears are open unto their prayers: but the face of the Lord is against them that do evil."

"But," you ask, "doesn't a Christian sometimes make a sinful step?" Yes, it is possible for a Christian to make a sinful step, but no Christian will make a sinful *walk*. If a Christian is making a sinful walk, he is no Christian at all. "If we confess our sins, he is faithful and just to forgive us our sins, and to cleanse us from all unrighteouness." Remember this always: *instant confession* means *constant fellowship*.

THE BRAZEN LAVER

Why do you suppose God placed the Brazen Laver, with the water in it, directly in front of the entrance to the Holy Place? Why was the Laver made of the looking glasses of the women, unless so that any of God's priests, including you, could pause and see himself and judge himself before he dared to go into the Holy Place of God and have communion with the Creator of the universe? Notice that, in the providence of God, where there is judgment, there is also mercy waiting right there for you, because, the thing that judged you would be the reflection of yourself in the Brazen Laver; and the very thing that judged you would also provide the water for your cleansing! There is no need for you to go into the Holy Place without this cleansing. Stay out of the Holy Place unless you cleanse yourself before you enter. Look at yourself in all honesty, and reflect on the fact that if a thing is not good, it is bad, that if it is not right, it is wrong. If it is not straight, it is crooked. If it is not clean, it is dirty. If dishonesty is dishonesty, call it that and repent. If impurity is impurity, call it that and repent. If holding back money from God in tithes and offerings is robbing God, call it robbery and go and sin no more. If you will not call it robbery, God will. If you will not judge it, God will, and He gives you a severe judgment on that in Malachi 3:8-10: "Will a man rob God? Yet ye have robbed me. But ye say, Wherein have we robbed thee? In tithes and offerings. You are cursed with a curse: for ye have robbed me, even this whole nation. Bring ye all the tithes into the storehouse, that there may be meat in mine house, and prove me now herewith, saith the Lord of hosts, if I will not open you the windows of heaven, and pour you out a blessing, that there shall not be room enough to receive it."

If the Christians of America had not robbed God unmercifully, we could have sent many more missionaries to Japan with the blessed Gospel. And the missionaries of Japan insist that had we increased our missionaries to Japan we would not now have to send our sons and daughters there on errands of death.

God is not to be trifled with. Either a revival must come to America or this country is doomed. Joseph Stalin declares that we are no longer a Christian nation, and the *World Almanac* statistics show that only 48 per cent of the people of America belong to any kind of Christian organization whatsoever, Catholic or protestant. If not for the sake of the red blood of Calvary, then in God's name and for the sake of the red, white and blue of the Star Spangled Banner, Christians of America, awake, cleanse yourselves and go into the Holy Place and commune with God!!

If you will not stop at the Brazen Laver and judge yourselves, do not dare to come into the Holy Place and commune with God. You are a dirty priest. There is no communion place for you in the Holy Place. Your prayers are not heard. There is no bread for you. There is no light for you from the Golden Candlestick. You are unclean, and you will add to your misery tenfold if you go into the Holy Place in that condition. You are obliged to stay outside the Holy Place. You can have the natural light of the sun by day, or the moon by night, but the light from the Golden Candlestick is not for you. You can get all the light you can possibly wrest from the philosophers. But you will get no light from Christ and no food from Christ. You will carry that heavy burden of doubts which you have been carrying so long, and will continue to carry to your grave, unless you "walk in the light, as he is in the light." "If we walk in the light, as he is in the light, we have fellowship one with another, and the blood of Jesus Christ his Son cleanseth us from all sin."

When we walk with the Lord
In the light of His Word,
What a glory He sheds on our way!

While we do His good will,
He abides with us still,
And with all who will trust and obey.

Not a shadow can rise,
Not a cloud in the skies,
But His smile quickly drives it away;
Not a doubt or a fear,
Not a sigh nor a tear,
Can abide while we trust and obey.

Not a burden we bear,
Not a sorrow we share,
But our toil He doth richly repay;
Not a grief nor a loss,
Not a frown nor a cross,
But is blest if we trust and obey.

Trust and obey,
For there's no other way
To be happy in Jesus,
But to trust and obey.

There you have God's recipe for absolute faith. A straight line is the shortest distance between two points. Do not swerve around that Brazen Laver. Pass close to it. Bathe in it, and then see what becomes of your doubts. Judge yourself so that God will not have to judge you.

"David, king of Israel, what is that I hear you say? 'Restore unto me the joy of thy salvation'? What, David? What is that? Where is the Twenty-third Psalm? Where are your green pastures? Where are your still waters?" asks his conscience.

"No more," answers David. "No more."

"How long since you have known that joy of salvation, David?"

"Oh, a very long time," cries the Psalmist.

"But how long is it, David? Can't you remember when you lost this joy?"

The great King David begins to weep and he mumbles, "Ever since Bathsheba . . . ."

"So Bathsheba is the name of the woman with whom you commited adultery," says David's conscience. The king cries in anger from his throne, and declares that he makes the social laws, that, as king, he can do no wrong, and that what may be wrong for others is permissible for him.

"So," inquires David's conscience, "you won't call that adultery?"

"No."

"Furthermore, there's that little matter of Bathsheba's husband, Uriah. Remember him, David? He is the captain you murdered."

"No, I didn't murder Uriah. I didn't. I didn't. Uriah was killed in battle. He was a soldier. Soldiers die every day."

"But Uriah didn't need to die on that particular day. You knew the very hour he was going to die. It was you, David, who ordered Uriah's little company to go up close to the walls, with the enemies shooting stones and arrows, much, much closer than was necessary, and with a much smaller company than he should have had. And wasn't it you, David, who gave the command to the trumpeter to stand just far enough away so that when the signal for retreat was given the brave Uriah would not hear the trumpet and would stay there by the wall to be annihilated with his entire group? That's the way it worked out, David, but you did give your comrade-in-arms a pompous military funeral. You did weep crocodile tears over his bier. All that you did, David. But you have never known one minute of joy or peace with God from that hour until the present."

Now Conscience slips closer to David and whispers in his ear. "So you'd like this joy of salvation again, would you, David?"

"Yes, yes," cries the king, brokenhearted and sobbing.

"How long since you have enjoyed a sermon from the Word of God, David?"

"Never since Uriah and Bathsheba . . ." cries the king. "Never since then I have I known a moment of peace?"

"Will you listen to the Word of God now, David? Shall I tell Nathan the prophet to come in and discuss the Word of God with you? Can you take it, David?"

"Yes, yes," cries the king. "I'm not that bad. Bring in the messenger of the most high God."

Now Nathan the prophet comes in. (You will find the essence of this episode in II Samuel 12.) Nathan begins, "O David, King of Israel, live forever. There was a rich man, King David, who had a palace and many sheep and cattle, and much goods, and there was a poor man who had only one little ewe lamb, that was like unto him as a daughter. It ate out of the same plate, drank out of the same goblet, and slept upon the same couch. It was all the poor man had.

"There came a time when the rich man wanted to make a feast for a traveler who came through the country. And what did the rich man do? Did he take one of his many sheep and cattle and kill it and roast it for the feast? No, the rich man didn't do that. What did the rich man do? He went down to the poor man's house and took the little ewe lamb away from the poor man and killed it for the feast. What do you think of a man like that, David?" asks Nathan.

And David rises in judgment (even as you and I would) upon the other fellow (and never for a moment thinks to judge himself). The self-righteous David hurls down the condemnation, "Such a man is not fit to live."

Like a flash of lightning Nathan the prophet points an accusing finger at the king and cries, *"Thou art the man."*

Notice how consistent the Bible is. The prophet Nathan continues and in substance says, "But God has put away your sin; you shall not die. But because you have done this thing, your baby boy will die, and your other son Absolom will rise up to be a curse to you; you will never build the holy Temple, and blood will never depart from your house. Thus saith the Lord. Good-bye."

David could have avoided much grief if only he had judged himself, and had not waited for the great and holy God to judge him. When you wait too long, God gives the judgment, and with the judgment comes the chastisement, "that we should not be condemned with the world."

Pause long and steadily, and look at yourself in that Brazen Laver. Then bathe freely in the cleansing water, for Christ is not only our Saviour, as we see at the Brazen Altar of Sacrifice, He is our Purifier, He is our Life, He is our Intercessor, He is our Bread.

Then look somewhere else after you have seen the reflection of yourself in the Brazen Laver. Look at all the furniture, from the head of the cross in the Holy of Holies to the arms of the cross in the Holy Place, to the Brazen Altar of Sacrifice at the foot of the cross. Look long and wonderingly at the Cross of the Christ and at the Christ of the Cross, for Whosoever looks upon Him shall be healed. A look at Christ will spoil you for covetousness. A look at Christ will spoil you for dishonesty. A look at Christ will spoil you for adultery. A look at Christ will spoil you for meanness and cheapness.

> See from His head, His hands, His feet,
>   Sorrow and love flow mingled down;
> Did e'er such love and sorrow meet,
>   Or thorns compose so rich a crown?

BLOOD AND WATER

"One of the soldiers with a sword pierced his side, and forthwith came out blood and water." I am glad that the beloved John noticed the water, as well as the blood, coming from the side of our blessed Lord. I am convinced that God placed the Brazen Laver, containing water mingled with blood, at the lower center of the cross because He was thinking of the water and the blood that would flow from the side of Christ. The Bible is always thousands of years ahead of science, and I am glad John noticed the water flowing with the blood, because it points to a tender and wonderful probability namely, that the Lord Jesus Christ died of a broken heart.

Dr. Simpson, the discoverer of chloroform, wrote a brochure showing what happens in the case of a broken heart. He declares, "The human heart is enclosed in a pericardium which contains lymph, or water, which acts as a lubricant, or cushion, for the heart itself. The only time that water and blood run together from an external cut in the human body is when this pericardium breaks. The patient," says Dr. Simpson, 'in a case of heartbreak, throws back his arms as far as they will go. The body is stiffened out as far as possible. There is a loud cry, and the pericardium breaks, and then, and only then, do the lymph and the blood flow together."

Blood and water flowed from our precious Lord's riven side. His body was stiffened. His blessed arms were thrown as far apart as the cursed nails would let them go. There was a loud cry, "It is finished." Is it not probable that His heart broke?

Before you dare commune with Him, before you dare accept any light or food from Him at the Holy Place, stand by the Brazen Laver and cry, "Search me, O God, and know my heart . . . and see if there be any wicked way in me, and lead me in the way everlasting." Then reach deep into your own heart, and whatever the Holy Spirit shows you should not be there, if you value your salvation, if you value your communion with the Lord God, then reach down and pull that thing from the bottom of your heart, and lay it at the foot of the Cross.

"I beseech you therefore, brethren, by the mercies of God, that ye present your bodies a living sacrifice, holy, acceptable unto God, which is your reasonable service" (Romans 12:1).

"If we walk in the light, as he is in the light, we have fellowship one with another, and the blood of Jesus Christ his Son cleanseth us from all sin" (I John 1:7).

Printed in the United States of America